22-16

20-16

BLOCK

1-16

No 1

1-16

PLEASE
RETURN
THIS
BOOK
TO
SOMEONE
ELSE

32-16

*Block*

Chevette

32-16    1

Baberton
Junior

43-16

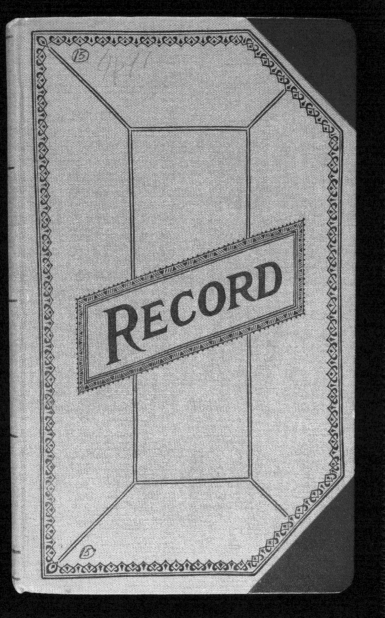

RECORD

16-16

BLUELINE

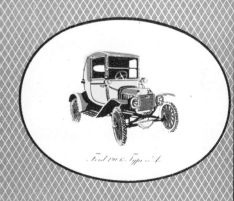

26-16

26-16

Everybody knows that the game is crooked
                    but everybody plays
Everybody knows that the dice are loaded
                    but everybody (rolls) prays
Everybody knows that the fight is fixed
that the poor stay poor and the rich get
                                        rich

That's how it goes
Everybody knows


Every single breath that I take
Every crust of bread that I break

"[THE ARCHIVE] IS AT THE VERY CENTER OF
THE THING. I SEE THE WORK FLOATING
ON THE MATERIAL. [THE PUBLISHED SONGS
OR POEMS ARE] JUST THE BEACON, THE
DESIGNATION—SOMEHOW THE SIGNAL FOR
AN INVESTIGATION OF THE ENTIRE WORK...
THE ARCHIVE IS THE MOUNTAIN, AND THE
PUBLISHED WORK THE VOLCANO."

—Leonard Cohen

From Ira Nadel, "Introduction," *Various Positions:
A Life of Leonard Cohen* (New York: Knopf, 1996), 2–3.

# LEONARD COHEN

EDITED BY
Julian Cox and Jim Shedden

# EVERYBODY

INSIDE HIS ARCHIVE

# KNOWS

**AGO**

Delmonico · D.A.P.
New York

Texts by Alexander Arslanyan, Julian Cox,
Gillian McIntyre, and Jim Shedden, except where
otherwise noted.

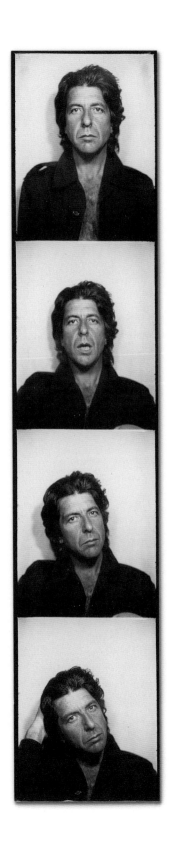

Leonard Cohen, *Self-Portrait Photo Booth*, c. 1975

## Director's Foreword

For over five decades, Leonard Cohen has had an immeasurable cultural influence internationally. From his first LP, *Songs of Leonard Cohen*, in 1967 at the age of thirty-three, to *You Want It Darker*, his final LP released in 2016, Cohen has been widely regarded as a popular music icon. At the same time, before embarking on his music career, Cohen had already established himself as a literary titan for his celebrated, and sometimes controversial, volumes of poetry and novels. In both his literature and his music, Cohen reflected on longing, sorrow, beauty, faith, life, and death.

Curated by the Gallery's Deputy Director & Chief Curator, Julian Cox, *Leonard Cohen: Everybody Knows* is a partnership with the Leonard Cohen Family Trust, and is the first museum exhibition to showcase the contents of Cohen's archive. This catalogue, and the exhibition that it documents, is primarily a visual journey through the archive, which Cohen considered to be his life's masterwork. Watercolours, sketchbooks, Polaroids, photo-booth selfies, letters, and other written and visual documents and personal items reveal details about Cohen's life and work that are less commonly known—or not known at all. While these pages are roughly chronological, the catalogue is neither a conventional biography nor a work of music history; instead, it takes its cues from the archive and delves into particular facets of Cohen's life and artistic output. The featured essays further support this approach by shedding light on Cohen's writing and music, in addition to his engagement with visual culture throughout his life.

For their exceptional support and collaboration, the AGO extends profound thanks to the Leonard Cohen Family Trust, including Robert Kory, Robert de Young, Ryan Kory, and Cheryl Cordingley; John Zeppetelli, Lesley Johnston, and the team at the Musée d'art contemporain de Montréal; Larry Alford, Loryl MacDonald, John Shoesmith, and Andrew Stewart at the Thomas Fisher Rare Book Library, University of Toronto; and Sharon Robinson, who co-wrote "Everybody Knows" with Cohen, for her steadfast support of and assistance with both the exhibition and publication in various ways. In addition, we thank our Signature Partner RBC, and Supporting Sponsors Shiseido (Canada) Inc. and Virgin Plus. For their lead support, we are grateful to the Dorothy Strelsin Foundation and an anonymous donor, as well as for the generous support of the Azrieli Foundation, the Bloomberg and Sen families, Greg & Susan Guichon, the Latner Family Foundation, and Janice Lewis & Mitchell Cohen, and additional support from the Birks Family Foundation and the DH Gales Family Foundation. The AGO also recognizes our exhibition Media Partner blogTO, Government Partner the Ontario Cultural Attractions Fund, and the Canada Council for the Arts, which provides support for contemporary art programming at the AGO. Without the ongoing commitment of our Development team to generate such support, we could not produce the high calibre of work that we do.

The AGO acknowledges the following lenders for enabling us to mount such an expansive collection of Cohen's creative property: Aviva Layton; Leonard Cohen Family Trust; Stephen Bulger Gallery; Thomas Fisher Rare Book Library, University of Toronto; and Musée d'art contemporain de Montréal, for the opportunity to showcase fantastic video works by contemporary artists George Fok and Kara Blake.

I commend our wonderful AGO staff for researching, coordinating, and mounting such an impressive and varied presentation, including the show's curator, Julian Cox; Jessica Bright, Chief, Exhibitions, Collections & Conservation; Laura Comerford, Associate Director of Exhibitions; Melissa Ramage, Project Manager; Gillian McIntyre, Interpretive Planner; Alex Arslanyan, Curatorial Research Assistant; Jill Offenbeck, Manager, Curatorial Affairs; Nives Hajdin, Editor; and Production Manager Malene Hjørngaard and her team, including Evelina Petrauskas and Theodora Doulamis for their graphic design and 3D exhibition design work respectively. For his intelligent and dynamic vision for this publication alongside Cox, as well as his invaluable subject matter expertise, I thank Jim Shedden, the AGO's Manager of Publishing, and his team. In addition, I have profound respect for our various catalogue contributors and their fascinating, intimate insights into the life of Leonard Cohen, including Cox, Shedden, Joan Angel, Laura Cameron, Robert Kory, Alan Light, and Michael Petit. For their generosity and support during the research stages of this project, we extended sincere thanks to Marsha Lee Berkman, Stephen Berkman, Linda Book, Ted East, Hazel Field, Bill Fury, Spring Hurlbut, Danielle Lindy, Kristina Ljubanovic, Alexandra Pleshoyano, and Michael Posner.

*Leonard Cohen: Everybody Knows* is a continuation of the Gallery's commitment to artists and creators who produce work in a variety of media. We are so fortunate to have collaborated with the Leonard Cohen Family Trust to present such an engrossing array of objects and artifacts that have been tucked away in Cohen's archive for years. We are thrilled to have this rare opportunity to provide our audiences with greater insight into one of Canada's most enigmatic cultural icons.

—

STEPHAN JOST
Michael and Sonja Koerner Director, and CEO

*return of the Polaroid Swinger*

rd Cohen, *Return of the Polaroid Swinger,* 1968

# SCALING THE MOUNTAIN

Julian Cox

Leonard Cohen was to the manor born. His family name—a variant of Kohen—translates as "high priest" in Hebrew, and his first name, Eliezer/Leonard, carefully chosen by his Jewish parents, means "God is my helper." The second child and first son born into a well-to-do family of rabbis, Talmudic scholars, and businessmen in Westmount, Montreal, Cohen was a *kohen* shaped by a compelling and convincing sense of destiny.[1] He would become someone and be sure to make a mark. From a young age he possessed a clear notion of his singular gifts, even if he persistently struggled to reconcile his bourgeois background with the vicissitudes of his artistic sensibility. As he evolved into a poet, songwriter, and charismatic troubadour, he presented a transparently unvarnished but deeply authentic persona—suave and urbane, and was gifted with a gravitas that transfixed his audience in public and private settings. Cohen was intentional in everything he did and a skilled navigator. He was purposeful about leaving a posthumous road map in the form of an archive. It was all part of the plan.

Cohen's instinct to gather and preserve—to assiduously assemble an archive—ran in parallel to his practice as a writer. He typically had a notebook, letter pad, or sheaf of papers on his person at all times, and he would often revisit the same quatrain, elastically revising the language until arriving at a point where the meaning or expression was right (fig. 1). At his neighbourhood synagogue, Shaar Hashomayim, a short walk across the park and down the hill from his childhood home, he imbibed the power of language, and its capacity to inspire and transport. He developed a love of language and reverence for Jewish religious symbolism and took them with him into his undergraduate studies at McGill University, where he emerged as a leader on the debate team. Here he first learned how to perform for an audience and take on multiple guises, gaining important insight into the art of self-portrayal. His comfortable upper-middle-class upbringing enfolded him in a cloak of confidence—that he would be a success was never in doubt. Mostly, the question was when, how, and in what profession.

Cohen's ascent was sharp, such that by the beginning of his third decade he was the subject of a documentary film, *Ladies and Gentlemen... Mr. Leonard Cohen,* created in 1965 for the National Film Board of Canada. The film profiles an artist on the rise and is inflected by Cohen's mildly absurdist and self-deprecating humour. One biographer, Sylvie Simmons, aptly describes *Ladies and Gentlemen* as "less a portrait of a serious literary figure than of a pop/rock celebrity in training."[2] Toward the end of the film, we see Cohen at his ironic best: sitting in a bathtub, he writes the words "*caveat emptor*" on the bathroom wall in a black marker—essentially sending the warning "let the buyer beware," and don't believe everything you see just because it is in a documentary. As portrayed in the film, Cohen's identity floats between bourgeois and bohemian. It is acutely apparent that he can embrace the mainstream and the counterculture with equal ease. An increasingly recognizable public figure, Cohen embodied these enigmatic tensions and strategically exploited them in his work as a writer and later as a singer-songwriter.

*Ladies and Gentlemen* features a carefully narrated voiceover by the film's co-director, Donald Brittain, which includes the statement: "Cohen collects his letters and makes certain he is heavily photographed. He does this simply because he feels he is becoming an important writer and that such material will someday be of value."[3] This conviction had already taken an explicit turn, through an initial sale of Cohen's papers to the University of Toronto in 1964. The vendor, Laurie Hill Limited, Montreal, described the offering as "a collection of the notebooks, journals, draft and final manuscripts, letters and first editions of this brilliant young Canadian writer.... The material in this collection not only covers Mr. Cohen's writing up to the present time but is rich in biographical material of inestimable future value."[4] Although additional tranches of material were transferred to the University of Toronto over the years,[5] Cohen held back the majority of his archive for his own use and reflection. It was primarily assembled at his home and business office in Los Angeles, and then transferred to the Leonard Cohen Family Trust for safekeeping after his death in 2016.

The archive as it now stands amounts to hundreds of photographs; prints and drawings; notebooks; voluminous quantities of personal and business correspondence; fan mail; musical instruments; touring merchandise; and Cohen's personal library. It provides rich glimpses into Cohen's multiple lairs—Montreal, Hydra, New York, Nashville, Mt. Baldy, and Los Angeles—and reveals the tremendous network of colleagues and fellow artists who were integral to the formation of Cohen's public identity and reputation. However, only a fraction of this material has hitherto been made available to scholars and researchers, and it has not been shown publicly. The exhibition and catalogue *Leonard Cohen: Everybody Knows* present to audiences for the first time a selection of objects, papers, and artifacts drawn from this archive. They surface an array of materials that provide fresh insight into the arc of Cohen's protean creative pursuits over six decades.

—

Cohen needed solitude but at the same time craved attention. Making photographs responded to both impulses, and he took to working with a Polaroid Swinger Model 20 Land Camera beginning in the fall of 1967.[6] This apparatus was portable and easy to use, its compact roll film accommodating eight exposures and generating prints that fit comfortably in the palm of the hand. The set-up of camera and film allowed the operator to explore an incremental and sustained attention to a specific subject. Its use could be intensely private, an advantage that allowed Cohen to be very deliberate about each picture. The development time for each exposure was so brisk that the results were at once immediate and indelible. The camera ejected the type 20 film with the positive and negative sandwiched together and, after about fifteen seconds, the user peeled them apart. To do this well required concentration and exactitude. A journal entry accompanying one self-portrait from 1968 (fig. 2) informs us that Cohen was not always a successful operator: "White scratches in the hair indicate technical incompetence with Polaroid Land Swinger Model 20." We know that he was persistent, because in the same notebook that Cohen used during visits to New York and Nashville between 1967 and 1969, it is apparent that photography and writing were integral to his daily regimen and practised symbiotically as forms of self-expression.

When on the road, Cohen would set up a worktable in his hotel room to serve as the anchor for his creative pursuits. His notebook records an entry on January 9, 1969, in room 217 of the Chelsea Hotel, New York City, next to a snapshot of his desk and typewriter with a note that reads: "a rare and much-loved work table in the life of the author." Another talismanic photograph, this from his room at the Noelle Hotel, Nashville, shows a harvest of Polaroids from a session of intensive shooting (fig. 3). Here we see the self-contained activity of the artist-writer in retreat. More than twenty Polaroids are scattered across the table, suggesting the extent of Cohen's preoccupation with recording and image-making. A big part of this was his obsession with self-care and body image (a lifelong fixation), continually focused on a distillation of his corporeal and spiritual

Sunday November 3

She gave me half a walnut. It looked like a tiny brain.

She gave me half a shelled walnut. Corregated, perfect, it looked like a tiny brain.

She gave me a shelled half of a walnut. Corregated, perfect, it looked like a tiny brain.

She put a tiny brain in my hand. It was half of a perfect shelled walnut.

Fig. 1 Leonard Cohen, *Diary Entry about a Walnut,* c. 1960

Fig. 2 Leonard Cohen, *White Scratches in the Hair Indicate Technical Incompetence with Polaroid Land Swinger Model 20,* 1968

Fig. 3 Leonard Cohen, *Forlorn Harvest,* 1968

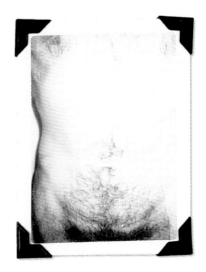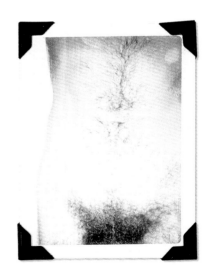

Fig. 4 Leonard Cohen, *Nude Torso,* 1968–1969

Fig. 5  Leonard Cohen, *Unified Heart
and Chinese Symbols Stamps,* date unknown

Fig. 6  Suzanne Elrod, *Acapulco,* 1971

landscape toward its essence.[7] A pair of close-up self-portrait views of his torso (fig. 4) is accompanied by the inscription: "Still wake up dead but body improving with daily exercise; morning somewhat tolerable with devotion to this book."

This attention to ritual and the observance of daily habits was in part shaped by Cohen's multi-faith perspective. He was first and foremost Jewish but sought wisdom, solace, and companionship in a multitude of spiritual teachings. Cohen's yearning for ascetic growth and curiosity for new ways of experiencing the world played out in his exploration of the I Ching, Christianity, especially Catholicism, Scientology, Zen Buddhism, and Hinduism. He drew inspiration from each as sources for his writing and performing; he accompanied many of his later self-portraits with stamps of two symbols that reflect the breadth of his spiritual ideals (fig. 5). The first stamp represents the Order of the Unified Heart, signifying love, harmony, and faith in humanity through a design that alludes to the Star of David but with softened edges and two interwoven hearts. It is welcoming to all. The second stamp is a Chinese aphorism presented in two aspects: the left side signifying the ego, the self, and the "I"; and the right side standing for the good-natured, fair-minded character. The stamps—which he used widely, incorporating them in his later prints and publications—reflect Cohen's hope for a lasting humanity and deftly meld his present concerns with traditions from the past.[8]

Repeatedly throughout his career as a recording artist, Cohen incorporated photographs from his archive as elements of the artwork for his albums and printed publications. He did so with great intentionality, understanding the totemic power of photography and its utility as a representational tool. One of Suzanne Elrod's photographs of Cohen (fig. 6), made during a trip to Acapulco in 1971, was deployed on the back cover of his collection of poems *The Energy of Slaves* (1972) and on the front cover of *Leonard Cohen: Live Songs* (1973). Meanwhile, his lifelong interest in drawing was mostly kept private until 2007, when a trio of exhibitions shared examples of his work in a variety of media—napkin doodles, pastels, watercolours, charcoal sketches, and digital images produced by drawing on a computer tablet.[9] Although he had no desire to seek recognition for being a visual artist, nor to be remembered as one, the profusion of drawings and sketches in his archive affirms the centrality of visual art to his creative pursuits. Cohen's artwork was employed robustly in *Book of Longing* (2006) and posthumously in *The Flame: Poems and Selections from Notebooks* (2018).

As part of his process of artistic discovery, Cohen preserved all his work in its various stages. He revised his writing obsessively, fine-tuning a verse or a sentence until its shape satisfied. Cohen himself positioned his archive as being "at the very center of the thing. I see the work floating on the material. [The published songs or poems are] just the Beacon, the designation—somehow the signal for the investigation of the entire work.... The archive is the mountain, and the published work the volcano."[10] In its depth and breadth, the archive shows the many roads taken, revealing more the journey than the destination. Unmistakably, it demonstrates Cohen's tireless will to create. He may not have considered his life's expedition as prospecting for gold, but he delivered it anyway.

—

JULIAN COX is the Deputy Director and Chief Curator at the Art Gallery of Ontario. His prior curatorial appointments include positions at the Fine Arts Museums of San Francisco, the High Museum of Art, Atlanta, and the J. Paul Getty Museum, Los Angeles. He is the author of numerous articles and publications, most recently *Matthew Wong: Blue View* (2021).

—

1. Several biographies chronicling Cohen's life are available: Ira Nadel, *Various Positions: A Life of Leonard Cohen* (New York: Knopf, 1996); Sylvie Simmons, *I'm Your Man: The Life of Leonard Cohen* (Toronto: McClelland & Stewart, 2012); and, most recently, Michael Posner, *Leonard Cohen, Untold Stories*, vol. 1, *The Early Years* (Toronto: Simon & Schuster, 2020); *Leonard Cohen, Untold Stories*, vol. 2, *From This Broken Hill* (Toronto: Simon & Schuster, 2021); and *Leonard Cohen, Untold Stories*, vol. 3, *That's How the Light Gets In* (Toronto: Simon & Schuster, 2022).

2. Simmons, *I'm Your Man,* 137.

3. *Ladies and Gentlemen...Mr. Leonard Cohen*, directed by Donald Brittain and Don Owen (National Film Board of Canada, 1965), 44 min.; see min. 21:57.

4. The letter, dated July 10, 1964, was signed by Bernard Amtmann, a specialist in rare books and manuscripts for Laurie Hill Limited, Montreal. The letter is part of the Leonard Cohen Papers at the Thomas Fisher Rare Book Library, University of Toronto. Many thanks to Loryl MacDonald, associate chief librarian for Special Collections and director, Thomas Fisher Rare Book Library, for sharing this reference with me.

5. In 1963, the University of Saskatchewan was the first public institution to approach Cohen to acquire his manuscripts and letters. After McGill University turned him down, he sold his papers to the University of Toronto. The first transaction in 1964 was for the sum of $3,850; a second followed in 1966 for $5,700. Additional materials were transferred in subsequent years.

6. The Polaroid Swinger Model 20 was released in 1965 and was a great success for the Polaroid Corporation. It was the first of several Polaroid cameras Cohen had over the course of his life. He also prolifically used the Polaroid SX-70 Land Camera, which was introduced in 1972.

7. As a young boy, Cohen struggled with his weight, and as he passed into adulthood he cultivated a careful routine to maintain a trim physique. This included yoga, meditation, and regular lap swimming. His obsession with appearance also informed his practice of fasting, which became at times almost ritualistic. After completing *Beautiful Losers* (1966), he embarked on a ten-day fast that left him utterly worn down.

8. See Joan Angel, "The Humble One: A Polyptych of Self-Portraits in *Book of Longing* and *The Flame*," in *The Contemporary Leonard Cohen*, ed. Kait Pinder and Joel Deshaye (Waterloo: Wilfrid-Laurier University Press, forthcoming).

9. The first of the exhibitions was held at the Richard Goodall Gallery, Manchester; the second, *Drawn to Worlds: Visual Works from 40 Years*, at the Drabinsky Gallery, Toronto, as part of the Luminato Festival; the third, *Leonard Cohen: Art Works*, at LindaLando Fine Art, Vancouver. For a review of the Vancouver exhibition, see Fiona Morrow, "My Old Man's New Medium," *Globe and Mail*, December 3, 2008, theglobeandmail.com/arts/my-old-mans-new-medium/article664282/.

10. Quoted in Nadel, *Various Positions,* 2–3.

Leonard Cohen, *Guide to the Notebooks: Book 1, Mt Baldy*, 1994

# INSIDE HIS ARCHIVE

In 1934, Leonard Cohen was born into a wealthy family of rabbis, Talmudic scholars, and businessmen in Westmount, Montreal. His family name translates to "high priest" in Hebrew, and from an early age Cohen was shaped by a compelling sense of destiny and a confidence in his singular gifts. He had a comfortable upbringing, attending Hebrew day school and summer camps in rural Quebec and Ontario. At his neighbourhood synagogue, Shaar Hashomayim, he hungrily absorbed the power of language, and its capacity to inspire and transport, while passionately seeking out spirituality in all its forms.

His father, Nathan, died when Leonard was only nine years old, leaving his mother, Masha, widowed, and his older sister, Esther, bereaved on the eve of her thirteenth birthday. Nathan had bequeathed his leather-bound poetry library to his son, in which Leonard lost himself as a way to numb his grief.

Nathan Cohen,
*Cohen Family Home Movies*, 1930s–1940s

Leonard and Esther Cohen riding bikes,
*Cohen Family Home Movies*, 1930s–1940s

Leonard Cohen and family dog,
*Cohen Family Home Movies*, 1930s–1940s

Esther and Leonard Cohen in front of family house with dog,
*Cohen Family Home Movies*, 1930s–1940s

## Cohen Family Home Movies, 1930s–1940s

These stills, derived from Cohen family home movies and mostly likely shot by Cohen's father, provide a glimpse of Cohen's carefree childhood with his sister, Esther, growing up in the affluent Montreal neighbourhood of Westmount. The comfort and privilege of their upbringing is evident as a parade of well-dressed family members appear on camera. The family dog, a black Scottish terrier named Tovarich ("comrade" in Russian), was a birthday gift to Leonard from his parents. He fictionalized this period of his life in his 1963 debut novel, *The Favourite Game*.

## Masha Cohen

Born Kaunas, Lithuania, 1905
Died Montreal, Canada, 1978

Masha Cohen (Kline) was born to a family of Russian Jews living in Kaunas, Lithuania, then part of the Russian Empire. Her father, Solomon Klonitzky-Kline, was a celebrated Hebrew scholar and rabbi who wrote the 700-page *Ozar Taamei Hazal: Thesaurus of Talmudic Interpretations*. In 1926, the family fled Kaunas as a rising tide of anti-Semitism grew in Eastern Europe. Masha immigrated to Canada and began work as a nurse for the Red Cross. In 1927, Masha married Nathan Cohen; the couple had two children, Esther and Leonard. Masha and Leonard had an intensely involved mother-son relationship.

*Esther and Leonard Cohen walking dog, Cohen Family Home Movies, 1930s–1940s*

*Leonard Cohen playing hockey, Cohen Family Home Movies, 1930s–1940s*

Unknown photographer, *Masha Cohen*, c. 1940

## My Sister's Birthday, 1961

This unpublished semi-autobiographical account stoically describes a nine-year-old boy, Leonard, and his twelve-year-old sister, Esther, learning of their father's death, and the grim rites that take place on what happens to be the eve of her thirteenth birthday. The final sentence on the second page reads: "I remember looking in the large dictionary for another word for 'happy.'"

Leonard Cohen
599 Belmont Ave
Montreal 6
Canada
Page 1

### My Sister's Birthday
#### by Leonard Cohen

We did not think our father would die, my sister nor I. He had been to the hospital many times before for his heart. Our only fear was that he would not be back from the hospital until after the plums had ripened. There were slender plum trees planted along the iron fence of our front lawn. When it was time, and only our father knew that time, when the plums were round and dusty, my sister and I would pick them, standing on white step-ladders, while he supervised from a little way back, calling out when here or there we missed a cluster.

"I'm afraid it's almost time," I told my sister one morning as we descended the stairs to breakfast.

Cohen     Page 2

"You've said that every morning this week," replied my sister in the bored voice appropriate to her seniority. She was twelve, three years older than I. "Don't worry."

Nursie was seated solemnly at the breakfast table, her hands folded on the white cloth before her like a school-girl's. She greeted us good morning but did not speak again during the meal. When we were finished the door to the kitchen was mysteriously closed and the maid did not remove the dishes. "You will not go to school this morning, my poor children. Your poor father passed away very late last night. Your mother is still sleeping and we must be all of us very quiet."

"You mean he's dead? our father's dead?" implored my sister.

"The funeral will be tomorrow, my poor children."

"O Nursie," and we both rushed to her arms.

"I wanted you to eat your breakfasts first."

"It can't be tomorrow," I protested, my face in her shoulder, "it's my sister's birthday."

She hugged us tighter.

Neither Nursie nor I wished my sister Happy Birthday the next morning. It wasn't something you said on the day of a funeral. I remember looking in the large dictionary for another word for 'happy.'

Leonard Cohen, *My Sister's Birthday*, c. 1960

Beginning in 1946, Cohen spent several summers at Camp Wabikon on Lake Temagami, about 250 miles north of Toronto. He thrived in outdoor sports as well as in social activities such as singing by the campfire and storytelling. His time there proved to be a formative experience. In this letter to his mother, Cohen describes his delight at catching a fish and remarks that he is writing lots of letters. Camp Wabikon features prominently in the closing chapters of *The Favourite Game.*

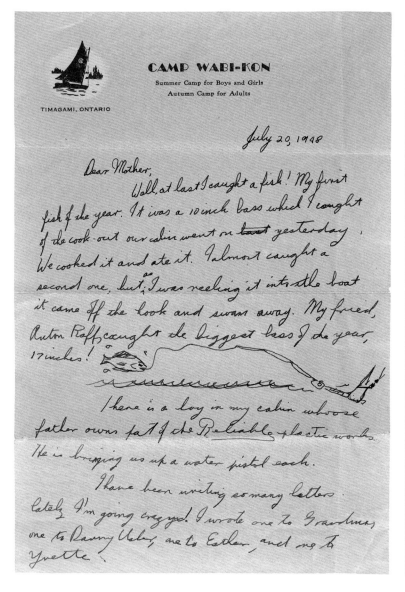

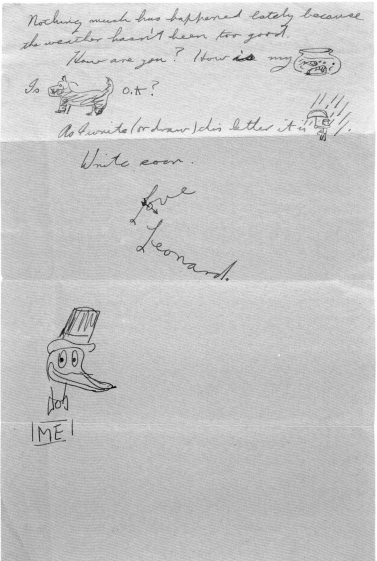

Leonard Cohen, *Camp Wabikon*, 1948

While studying at McGill University, Leonard Cohen befriended two of his professors, Irving Layton and Louis Dudek, who guided his growth as a poet. Through their encouragement, Cohen won the McGill University Poetry Prize for his poem "Sparrows," which was then published on the front page of the *McGill Daily*. Cohen was also published in three issues of *CIV/n*, a poetry journal spearheaded by Dudek, Layton, and others.

### The Buckskin Boys

While studying at McGill, Cohen was active in Hillel, a Jewish student organization, and also acted in plays and joined the Hillel band. In 1952, Cohen also founded a country and western trio called the Buckskin Boys, featuring himself on guitar, Mike Doddman on harmonica, and "Terry" on bucket bass. Cohen had a deep interest in country music, and it had a major influence on his music throughout his career.

FROM TOP LEFT
(clockwise):

Unknown photographer, *Leonard Cohen at the Gates of McGill,* c. 1953

Unknown photographer, *Leonard Cohen with the Buckskin Boys,* c. 1953

Unknown photographer, *Leonard Cohen (back, holding a guitar) and Mort Rosengarten (right, holding a trombone) with the Hillel Band at McGill University,* 1954

—

OPPOSITE PAGE,
FROM TOP LEFT
(clockwise):

Cover of *CIV/n* no. 5, 1954

Leonard Cohen, "Satan in Westmount" in *CIV/n* no. 5, 1954

Sadie Cantor, *Aviva Layton, Irving Layton, Georgianna Sherman (Anne), and Leonard Cohen in the Laurentians, Quebec,* 1957

11.

LEONARD NORMAN COHEN

### Satan In Westmount

One noticed his hands
finely carved
almost the colour of jade
and the fingernails
pink and cultivated
    He spoke of art
      and of poetry
      and held us with descriptions
    of the Masters
Often when walking
he sang fragments
of austere Spanish songs
from the Court of Ferdinand
and quoted Dante
accurately and often
    But in his lapel
    discreetly
    he wore a sprig of asphodel

### Folk Song

The ancient craftsman smiled
  when I asked him to blow a bottle
  to keep your tears in.
And he smiled and hummed in rhythm with his hands
  as he carved delicate glass
  and stained it with purple
  of a drifting evening sky.
But the bottle is lost in a corner of my house.
How could I know you could not cry?

### Les Vieux

Northeastern Lunch,
  with rotting noses and tweed caps,
huddling in thick coats
and mumbling confidential songs
to ancient friends -
  the public men of Montreal:

and in parks
  with strange children
who listen to sad lies
in exchange for whistles
  carved from wet maple branches;

## Irving Layton (Israel Pincu Lazarovitch)
Born Târgu Neamț, Romania, 1912
Died Montreal, Canada, 2006

Irving Layton was a prolific poet whose work significantly influenced the landscape of 20th-century Canadian literature. Layton garnered national and international recognition for his work and helped fellow poets John Sutherland, Raymond Souster, and Louis Dudek cement Montreal as a creative-writing centre in the 1950s. At this time, he formed a close personal and professional relationship with Cohen, his junior by twenty years. Layton continued to write poetry until the early 1990s, when he was diagnosed with Alzheimer's.

*Let Us Compare Mythologies* is Cohen's first collection of poems, published in 1956 as part of the McGill Poetry Series and illustrated by Freda Guttman. This work was critically well received and propelled Cohen to revered status among Montreal's small community of poets. The collection includes many of the themes that Cohen continued to explore in his literary and songwriting pursuits, such as sex, death, love, and religion.

Leonard Cohen, *Let Us Compare Mythologies*, 1956

Six Montreal Poets, 1957
Cohen reads eight poems from *Let Us Compare Mythologies* on this
Folkways Records release.

Various artists, *Six Montreal Poets*, 1957

Often photographing himself in photo booths or with traditional portable cameras, Cohen was an early adopter of the instant photograph. He enjoyed the process and technology of photography and over the course of his life owned multiple cameras, including several different models of Polaroid. He photographed himself and those around him intensively. His self-portraits (of which there are hundreds) reveal his ever-present preoccupation with his appearance, which he carefully controlled.

Cohen's first serious love affair was with Georgianna Sherman, whom he called Anne or Annie. They met at Columbia University in New York City, where Cohen was pursuing graduate studies in literature and Sherman was a program coordinator. The innocence of their young love is captured in this gem-like framed photo-booth portrait.

FROM TOP LEFT
(clockwise):

Leonard Cohen,
*Self-Portrait,*
1957

Leonard Cohen,
*Leonard Cohen and
Morton Rosengarten,*
c. 1960

Leonard Cohen,
*Self-Portrait,*
1957

Leonard Cohen,
*Portrait of
Georgianna (Anne)
Sherman and
Leonard Cohen,*
c. 1958

Leonard Cohen, *Morton*, 1964

Morton Rosengarten grew up in close proximity to the Cohen family home in Westmount, Montreal. He became a lifelong friend of Cohen's after they met at Camp Hiawatha in the Laurentian Mountains during the summer of 1944. Rosengarten later became a sculptor and, in the 1950s, he and Cohen opened the Four Penny Gallery as a haven for contemporary poets and artists in Montreal. This expressive, rapidly drawn ink sketch is typical of the kind of drawings found in Cohen's notebooks from the period.

## A Jew Looks at Rembrandt

When young the Christians told me
how we pinned Jesus
like a lovely butterfly against the wood,
and I wept beside paintings of Calvary,
at velvet wounds and delicate,twisted feet—
until I saw his slaughtered ox
heavily hanging raw and wet orange
with spikes stuck in it.
Now their gentle accusations
intoxicate me with subtle,barbaric dreams
and I construct the cross before them
and lie about the strength and size of thorns.

You broke the thin highway
where I drove drunk
in a souped up tank
but you broke it
with your iron hairpin

Do you ever wonder
what these forests
are doing under my wheels

Crash crash the trees
sing as they fall
strafing against each other
like the hairy legs of crickets

Where was I going when
you snapped snapped it
like a thread in mother's teeth
I'll never know

Crash crash sing the trees
what a big forest
What a great tank
What strange pieces of a highway
snarled in my treads

Leonard Cohen,                    Leonard Cohen, "You Broke the Thin Highway," 1963

FROM TOP LEFT
(clockwise):

Unknown photographer,
*Leonard Cohen on Hydra*, 1961

Leonard Cohen, *Marianne Ihlen and
Axel Joachim Jensen Jr. on Hydra*,
c. 1963

Unknown photographer, *Three Good
Friends of Mine*, 1961–1964

Leonard Cohen, *Marianne Ihlen
with Donkey on Hydra*, 1961–1964

Unknown photographer,
*Leonard Cohen on Hydra II*, 1961

Leonard Cohen, *Leonard Cohen's
House on Hydra*, 1964

Unknown photographer,
*Leonard Cohen Dancing on Hydra*,
1961–1964

In 1959, Cohen received a Canada Council grant to fund a writing trip to Europe. He headed for Israel, followed by London, but after a few months he tired of the grey winter skies. He opted for warmer climes and ended up on the small Greek island of Hydra, where he became enamoured with a community of expat artists, writers, and intellectuals. It was here in May 1960 that he met and fell in love with Marianne Ihlen, who became one of his significant lovers and most influential muses.

When Cohen's grandmother left him $1,500, he used it to buy a house on Hydra—which had become a sanctuary for him—and lived there with Marianne and her son, Axel. For much of the 1960s, he divided his time between Hydra and Montreal. Hydra became central to Cohen's identity during that period, and he kept strong ties with the island for the rest of his life. (The Cohen family still owns and travels to the Hydra house to this day.)

Dear Mother,

I am settled in one of the most beautiful places I have ever seen, indeed it is one of the loveliest spots on our small world. It is the island of Hydra, 4 hours by boat from Athens. Hydra is a long, bare, high rocky island. It is an elegant view from the boat, the port, the waterside tavernas, the tall handsome houses, all built in the years around 1800. Some of these houses are stately and owned by powerful Greek families. They were built to withstand a siege - each has a bakery, storerooms, great cisterns for water (essential on this waterless island). I have rented a charming little house. It has 3 rooms full of sunlight, a terrace, a tiny outside kitchen and a primitive toilet. On my terrace there is a deep well from which I draw my water. The view is magnificent - the harbour and the blue Mediterranean. The walls are thick, 2½ feet of stone and whitewashed - so the rooms are always cool and pleasant. I even have an old bread oven built into one of my outside walls. The sky is generous - day after day there is sun and clear golden light. All over the rocks bloom a profusion of wild flowers, daisies, poppies, forget-me-nots. I get up at 7:30 every morning and work for 3 hours. Then I go down to the port for a breakfast of milk and bread and honey. Here is famous honey, the ancient poets sung about it. I sun + swim for a few hours, then I lunch on artichokes, cheese, roe and then the whole island goes to sleep for a few hours. I work for another two hours after siesta and then I wander down to the port to talk and watch the fishermen repair their nets and learn Greek. All in all life is orderly and sweet, always complying with the old ideal "a sound mind in a sound body". Love Leonard

Leonard Cohen, *Letter to Masha*, c. 1961

My darling Marianne,

Where are you?

The sun here is beautiful but it is not the Greek sun and the water has not the same depth of blue. But I don't ask any questions as I lie on the white sand and listen to my beard growing.

Cuba vibrates with energy. And this is just the beginning. All of South America is on the threshold of revolution. Sometimes I look at my poems and feel quite obsolete before the forces of history. People must eat. There must be an end to humiliation.

And what about you? Has the famous, brief, intoxicating Norwegian summer begun? Did Barnet finally get some hair?

Leonard Cohen, *Letter to Marianne*, 1961

March 10, 1962.

Dearest Marianne,

Your two letters came; a week has gone by since you were here; I am still in the Captain's strange house; the champagne is untouched; a mild day tricked me into smiles but it's winter again; I miss you and Canada and Greece, mostly you and sunshine, mostly you; I see the three of us in a house somewhere soon.

My editor has been sick this week so I haven't been able to consult him about the cuts I want to make - I don't think there will be more than a few weeks work if I get my way - but I suppose we'll thrash it out in a few days. I don't want to change the entire character of the book.

There are a million things I want to talk about with you, things I'm frightened about, things I'm happy about, but none of them really matter and oceans between us distort things that become very simple when we are together.

I spoke to Rosengarten on the phone and he told me his friend Kitty has bought a property on a beautiful desolate wild Canadian island, Bonaventure, and I told him to get me some land there too. We will all be Esquimaux and forget our manners and eat codfish and laugh at the weak and your long hair will get all shiney and thick with the grease of whales and Barnet will learn bad French in a country school.

I miss everything that I love. I long for you and blind love, brown bodies that speak to one another in a language we don't want to understand, I long for readers to devour my soul at a feast, I long for health in the sun, woods I know, tables of meat and fruit and bread, children shattering the monarchy of the home, I long for cities of preserved elegance and the chaotic quarters of modern cities where the village persists, for loyal restaurants, for parks and battles. I have so much affection for the world and you shall be my interpreter.

I want to get back to Canada and rob a bank.

All my love,

Leonard

Leonard Cohen, *Letter to Marianne II*, 1962

In the spring of 1961, soon after the Bay of Pigs crisis, Cohen made a trip to Cuba. This was his first journey to wartorn territories; he visited Israel during the Yom Kippur War of 1973 and then Ethiopia in 1974, during the Eritrean War of Independence. In this 1961 letter to Marianne Ihlen from Cuba, he writes: "Revolution is not hospitable to neurotic melancholy, which is just as a Revolution should be." Cohen was fascinated by firearms, military life, and the legacy of his father, who served as a lieutenant with the Canadian Expeditionary Force in World War I.

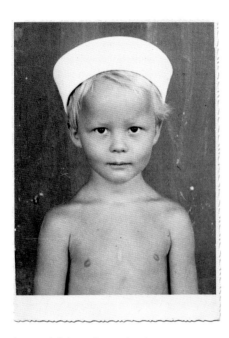

Leonard Cohen, *Portrait of
Axel Joachim Jensen Jr.*, 1964

## Marianne Ihlen

Born Lakollen, Norway, 1936
Died Oslo, Norway, 2016

Marianne Ihlen was a Norwegian model and Cohen's primary partner during the 1960s. She inspired many of his most famous songs, including "Bird on a Wire," "So Long, Marianne," and "Hey, That's No Way to Say Goodbye." They met in 1960 after Marianne separated from her husband, writer Axel Jensen, with whom she had a son, Axel Joachim Jensen.

In addition to the time they spent together on Hydra, Marianne accompanied Cohen on trips to Montreal and New York. During this period, Cohen acted as a surrogate father to Axel. Although his relationship with Marianne was fraught with infidelity and separation, the pair remained friends long after their romantic relationship ended.

Leonard Cohen, *Portrait of Marianne*, 1961–1964

Leonard Cohen, *Marianne Ihlen*, 1961–1964

_...la séparatisme!_

Sat. 25th

Dearest Leonidas,

This letter is a yelp for help! I've been rejected by Viking even tho' Cork S. said good things about my work + told me not to be too optimistic about the Children's editor. So, friend, please write by return mail + give me the name of your agent so I can get things in motion

again before summer. I still think the things are worth many more tries.

Wasn't it sad about losing my "bumble." It happened in St. Vincent's Hospital in N.Y. + when I emerged from anaesthetic, there was Annie like a pre-Raphaelite dream telling me that I was at home because Dylan Thomas had died there. Anyway, as I navig song, he always has to revise his masterpieces + we're working on it now — by next mail I ought to

Aviva Layton, _Airmail_, c. 1960

Laytons,
c/o Cousens,
R.R.I,
Eastman, P.Q.,
Canada!

Cohen
Hydra
Greece

VIA AIR MAIL

PAR AVION

Aviva Layton, _Airmail II_, c. 1960

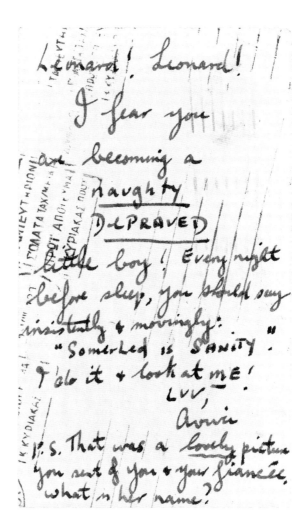

Aviva Layton, *Postcard from Aviva*, c. 1960

Aviva Layton, *Postcard from Aviva II*, c. 1960

## Aviva Layton

Born Sydney, Australia, 1933

Aviva Layton (Cantor) is a Canadian-American author of fiction, children's literature, and biography. She was Irving Layton's partner for twenty years, and the mother of David Layton (b. 1964). Because of the social mores of the day, Irving Layton was reluctant to leave his first wife, Betty Sutherland, for many years prior to eventually moving in with Aviva. While their secret relationship left Aviva quite isolated, Irving did introduce her to Cohen at that time, and the two connected personally and creatively. Aviva and Irving separated in the mid-1970s, while Cohen remained close with Aviva until his death in 2016.

Published in 1961, *The Spice-Box of Earth* was the most popular and commercially successful of Cohen's early books, and established his reputation as a leading poet in Canada. Its title draws from the ceremonial object—usually made of silver and decorated with elaborate filigree—used in the *havdalah* ("separation") ritual that marks the end of the Jewish Sabbath on Saturday evening. Cohen's poem

"Out of the Land of Heaven" celebrates the joy and sacredness of the Sabbath and the role of the spice box within it. This distinctive sketch made by Cohen, executed in ink on a scrap of cardboard, includes his family name—Kohen—written in Hebrew in the flag attached to the finial.

Leonard Cohen,
*The Spice-Box of Earth*,
1961

Leonard Cohen, *Spice Box of Earth*, c. 1960

Poem

Silence,
which to you
is near peace
than poems,
is to me
the drowning
of Icarus;
is to me
a crucifixion
done in Egypt.

And if,
for my gift
I brought you
silence
(for I know silence)
you would say:
This
is not silence,
this is
another poem—
and you
would hand it back
to me.

Leonard Cohen, "Gift," from *The Spice-Box of Earth*, c. 1960

Cohen's first novel was published in the United States by Secker and Warburg in 1963, after his Canadian publisher, Jack McClelland, found the autobiographical and sexual content too tedious and ultimately rejected it. McClelland & Stewart would eventually go on to publish it as well in 1970, and it has remained in print ever since. It is, perhaps, Cohen's *A Portrait of the Artist as a Young Man* or *The Catcher in the Rye*.

Leonard Cohen,
*The Favourite Game,*
1963

—

OPPOSITE PAGE:

Leonard Cohen,
*Flowers for Hitler,*
1964

Leonard Cohen,
*Flowers for Hitler,*
1964

Photo by John Max

**LEONARD COHEN** writes: "I was born in Montreal in 1934. I studied at McGill and Columbia Universities. Lived in London as a Lord, pursuing the fair, my accent opening the tightest Georgian palaces where I flourished dark and magnificent as Othello. In Oslo where I existed in a Nazi poster. In Cuba, the only tourist in Havana, perhaps in the world, where I destroyed my beard on the shores of Veradere, burnt it in nostalgia and anger for the Fidel I used to know. In Greece, where my Gothic insincerities were purged and my style purified under the influence of empty mountains and a foreign mate who cherished simple English. In Montreal, where I always return, scene of the steep streets which support the romantic academies of Canadian Poesy in which I was trained, seat of my family, old as the Indians, more powerful than the Elders of Zion, the last merchants to take blood seriously. I accept money from governments, women, poem sales, and if forced, from employers. I have no hobbies."

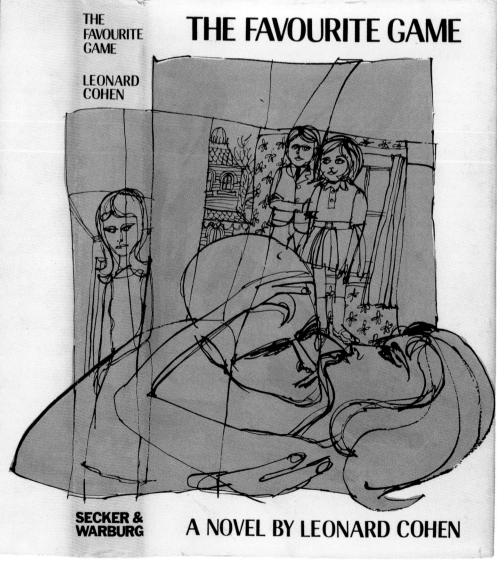

THE FAVOURITE GAME

LEONARD COHEN

THE FAVOURITE GAME

SECKER & WARBURG

A NOVEL BY LEONARD COHEN

Cohen's third volume of poetry moves away from the biblical references and romantic imagery of his first two books. According to literary scholar Nick Mount, "Instead of a falcon, the first poem references a mushroom cloud. There are poems about the Canadian parliament, Quebec separatists, and, of course, Hitler.... Many of the poems are about and/or affected by drugs, often wandering off into stoner surrealism."[1] The dedication that Cohen originally wrote but didn't use perhaps sums up the book's mood and essence most succinctly:

With scorn, love, nausea, and above all,
A paralysing sense of community
This book is dedicated
To the teachers, doctors, leaders of my
  parents' time:
THE DACHAU GENERATION[2]

Cohen wrote his second and final novel, *Beautiful Losers*, from 1964 to 1965 while living on Hydra, and it was first published in 1966. The complex, provocative, and visionary novel tells the story of three individuals who share a fascination with Catherine Tekakwitha, a seventeenth-century Mohawk saint, and who are also united by their sexual obsession and ultimately self-destructive hedonism. Although it was dismissed by many critics at the time, the book is now considered a classic of Canadian literature.

All of the copies of *Beautiful Losers* represented here are from the Thomas Fisher Rare Book Library, University of Toronto.

Leonard Cohen, *Beautiful Losers*, 1966

Leonard Cohen, *Beautiful Losers*, 1966

Leonard Cohen, *Beautiful Losers*, 1970

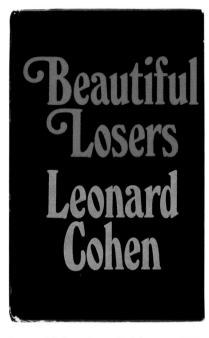

Leonard Cohen, *Beautiful Losers*, 1972

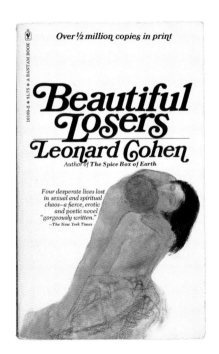

Leonard Cohen, *Beautiful Losers*, 1976

Leonard Cohen, *Beautiful Losers*, 1986

Leonard Cohen, *Beautiful Losers*, 1991

## Judy Collins

Born Seattle, Washington, United States, 1939

Judy Collins is a Grammy-winning singer-songwriter who rose to fame in the early 1960s in Greenwich Village, New York. Collins met Cohen through friends in 1966 while recording her sixth album, *In My Life*. Cohen presented his songs "Suzanne" and "Dress Rehearsal Rag" to Collins, who recorded her own versions, both of which appear on *In My Life*. Collins and Cohen formed a deep friendship that lasted well over forty years, with Cohen's songwriting appearing on eight different albums by Collins.

Judy Collins, *In My Life*, 1966

In the summer of 1966, Cohen headed to New York with the intent of continuing on to Nashville, where he thought he would become a professional country singer. Instead, he was attracted to the folk-rock sounds of Bob Dylan, Judy Collins, Joan Baez, and others, and decided to remain in New York, where he moved into the legendary Chelsea Hotel in 1967. In February 1967, Cohen made his musical debut at a benefit concert in the Village Theater, which would later become the Fillmore East. Perhaps due to nerves, Cohen walked off stage halfway through his first song, "Suzanne," but Judy Collins coaxed him back out and finished the song with him. Cohen performed numerous other gigs that year, notably at the Newport Folk Festival, the Mariposa Festival (Caledon, Ontario), and Expo 67 in Montreal.

By April 1967, Cohen had a contract with Columbia Records. Six months later, on December 27, 1967, *Songs of Leonard Cohen* was released, garnering both great acclaim and hostile dismissals. Over time, it has come to be appreciated as one of the most important records in popular music history. According to David and Lucy Boucher, "Cohen's meticulously crafted poems set to music, which owed more to French chanson and the guitar chord progression of Spanish Flamenco than to American roots music, nevertheless projected the darkness and shadowy edginess that were to be indelibly stamped on his projected image however hard he tried to escape it."[3]

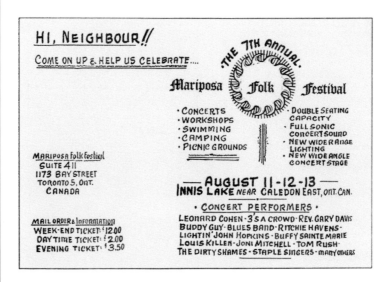

Mariposa Folk Festival poster, 1967

**CBS**
**RECORDS**

A Division of Columbia Broadcasting System, Inc.
51 West 52 Street
New York, New York 10019
(212) 765-4321

Dear Program Director:

The name Leonard Cohen is daily taking on new recognition! Over the past year Leonard Cohen has been acquiring new admirers and followers in enormous numbers. Many of the top established recording artists are picking up on his songs and recording them. "Suzanne" alone has been recorded by Noel Harrison, Judy Collins, the Inner Circle and others.

The continuously mounting sales on his Columbia album "Songs of Leonard Cohen," CS9533, is supporting evidence of the strength of Cohen as a writer and performing artist.

"Suzanne" was released earlier this year as a single. Since then the interest in the song and Leonard Cohen has excelled to such great heights that a reservice of this single has become mandatory!

The flip side is another example of Cohen's singing and writing ability. "Hey, That's No Way to Say Goodbye," also from the album, has been recorded by Judy Collins, Terry Ber, Julie Felix, Buffy Sainte-Marie, and others.

Take another listen to "Suzanne." This is the record, the artist, and the writer who is creating all the excitement....and airplay!

Please give this record the extra concentrated airplay that it deserves. I guarantee that Leonard Cohen and Suzanne, together, will really "turn your listeners on," to the record and to your station!

Thanks,

*Jim Brown*

Jim Brown
National Album Promotion Manager
JB:lf

In my 33rd year, in the month
of rainy June, I lived in New
York with a girl named Joan.
I was a student of Scientology
and she was singing at the Bitter
End. I grew to love her music. I
promised myself I would never
complain. We never seemed to eat
or sleep the the same time. She
lived on salads and veal parmigian
while I ate hot dogs and pizza
on the street. One morning she
didn't come back until seven thirty.
She had been with colourful friends.
While she was sleeping, line after line,
I wrote this following poem.

**max's**
**kansas city**
**steak lobster chick peas**

**wine list**

Leonard Cohen, *Max's Kansas City*, 1967

Max's Kansas City nightclub and restaurant was a famous hangout for the artists, writers, musicians, and other members of New York's intellectual and cultural elite. Andy Warhol's entourage, in particular, gathered in the backroom, where The Velvet Underground and Nico played regularly. Lou Reed recognized one of the patrons, Leonard Cohen, as the author of *Beautiful Losers,* and introduced him to Nico. Cohen was infatuated with the German singer, but she continuously rebuffed his advances. This poem, penned in June of 1967, details Cohen's life with a woman named "Joan."

To capitalize on the success of Cohen's first two albums, McClelland & Stewart published *Selected Poems, 1956–1968*. Cohen's first anthology comprised selections from his first four poetry volumes, plus an additional twenty poems partially selected by Marianne Ihlen. Over 200,000 copies were sold in the first three months alone. Cohen was awarded the Governor General's Award for English language poetry in Canada and famously refused to accept it, claiming, "Though much in me craves this award, the poems themselves absolutely forbid it."[4]

Leonard Cohen,
*Selected Poems, 1956–1968*,
1968

In September 1968, Cohen moved to a cabin in Franklin, Tennessee, with his partner Suzanne Elrod. He recorded material for his second album, *Songs from a Room*, in nearby Nashville while staying at the Noelle Hotel. During this time, Cohen kept a journal of photographs, poetry, and prose reflections on life, love, law, the body, and mortality.

Cohen strictly observed ritual and discipline. This notebook shows that photography and writing were integral to his daily routine as part of his exploration of self. To make the photographs, Cohen used a Polaroid Swinger Model 20 Land Camera, which was portable and easy to operate. Its compact roll film accommodated eight exposures and created prints that fit comfortably in the palm of the hand. Made for private viewing, the results are intimate and provide a compelling glimpse into Cohen's inner life at this pivotal moment of transition from writer-poet to singer-songwriter.

Leonard Cohen, *Tennessee Notebook* cover, 1968

View from the window
of Room 1221 Noel Hotel

Forlorn Harvest of Self-Portraits
Noel Hotel Rm 1221
December 18, 1968

The Jesus Calender purchased on 4th street in
front of Woolworths from old Rev. C.C. Haney
who caused it to be printed. 35¢. He told me
that he was getting his own radio program
in January. Asked me if I sung religious or
folklore. I liked him for the filthy ambitions
we shared in Nashville.

Leonard Cohen, *View from Window*, 1968

Leonard Cohen, *Forlorn Harvest*, 1968

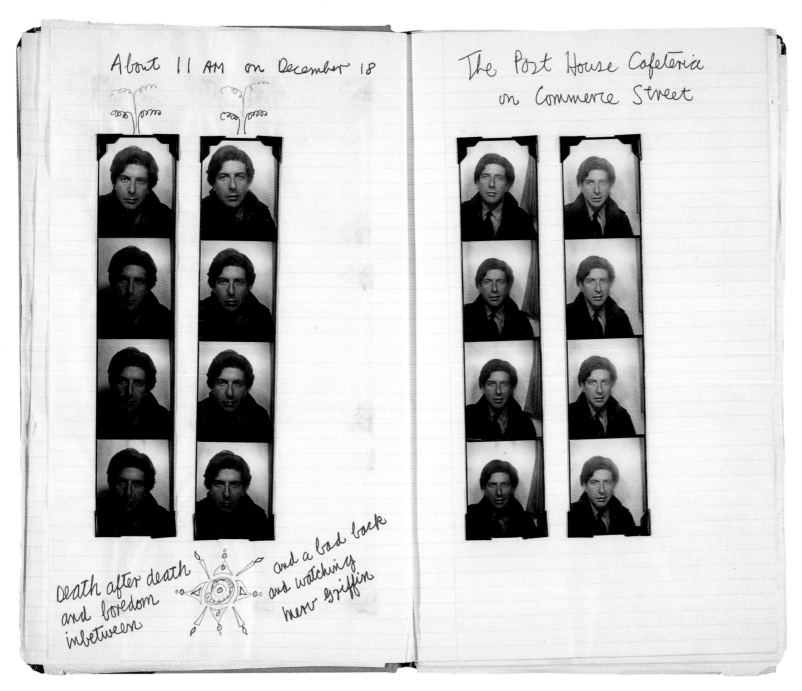

Leonard Cohen, *Death After Death*, 1968

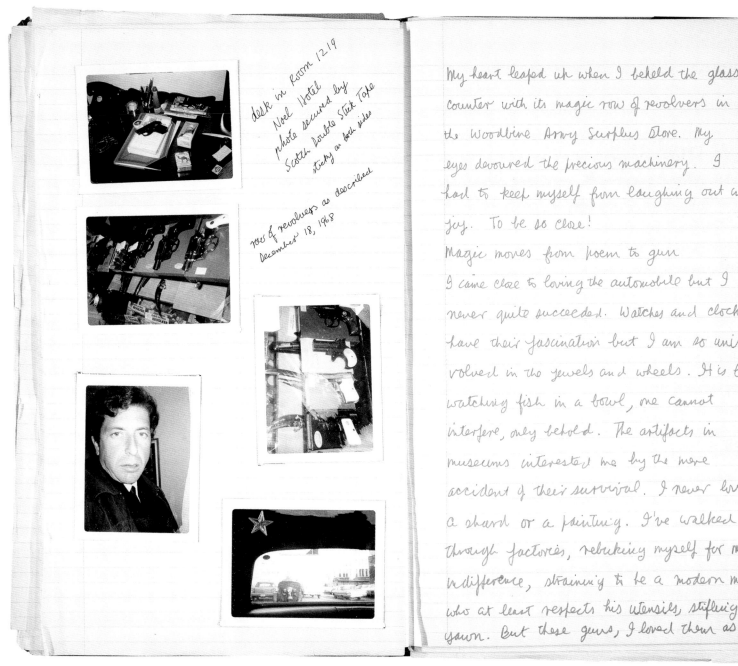

desk in Room 1219
Noel Hotel
photo secured by
Scotch Double Stick Tape
sticky on both sides

rows of revolvers as described
December 18, 1968

My heart leaped up when I beheld the glass counter with its magic row of revolvers in the Woodbine Army Surplus Store. My eyes devoured the precious machinery. I had to keep myself from laughing out in joy. To be so close!

Magic moves from poem to gun

I came close to loving the automobile but I never quite succeeded. Watches and clocks have their fascination but I am so uninvolved in the jewels and wheels. It is like watching fish in a bowl, one cannot interfere, only behold. The artifacts in museums interested me by the mere accident of their survival. I never loved a shard or a painting. I've walked through factories, rebuking myself for my indifference, straining to be a modern man who at least respects his utensils, stifling a yawn. But these guns, I loved them as

Leonard Cohen, *Desk in Room 1219*, 1968

application of penalties. This is symbolized by the terror of thunder. This clarity and severity have the effect of instilling respect; it is not that the penalties are ends in themselves. The obstructions in the social life of man increase when there is lack of clarity in the penal codes and slackness in executing them. The only way to strengthen the law is to make it clear and to make penalties certain and swift.

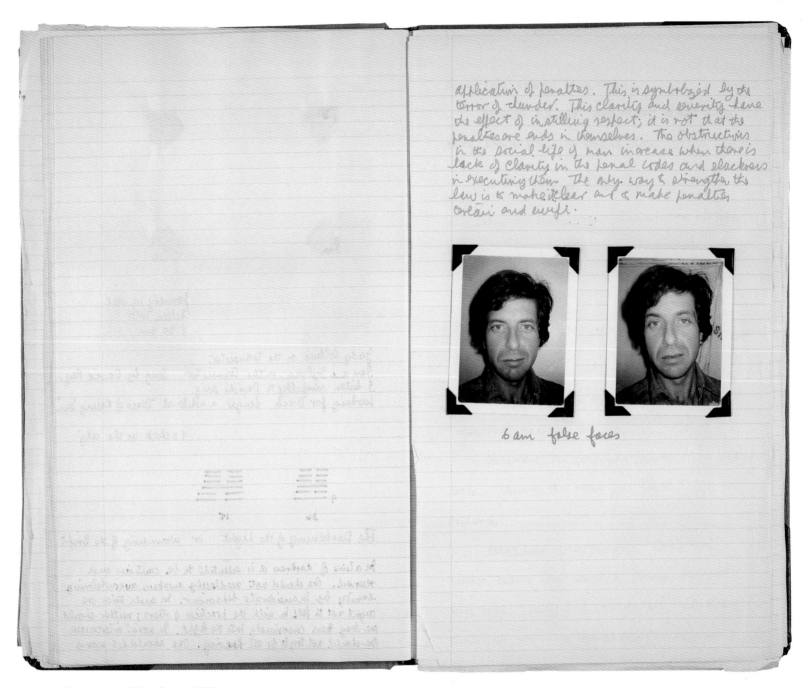

6 am false faces

Leonard Cohen, *6 am False Faces*, 1968

Leonard Cohen, *Self-Portraits and Cut-Out,* 1968

She yawned her tiny razor yawns with abandon, like one of ten thousand piranha stripping the thrashing horrified body of boredom.

She did not bother to mention, she did not know herself, that she had seen it before and was ready to try something else.

Look on, reader, at these ladies who are now dust and image alone.

Leonard Cohen, *She Yawned,* 1968

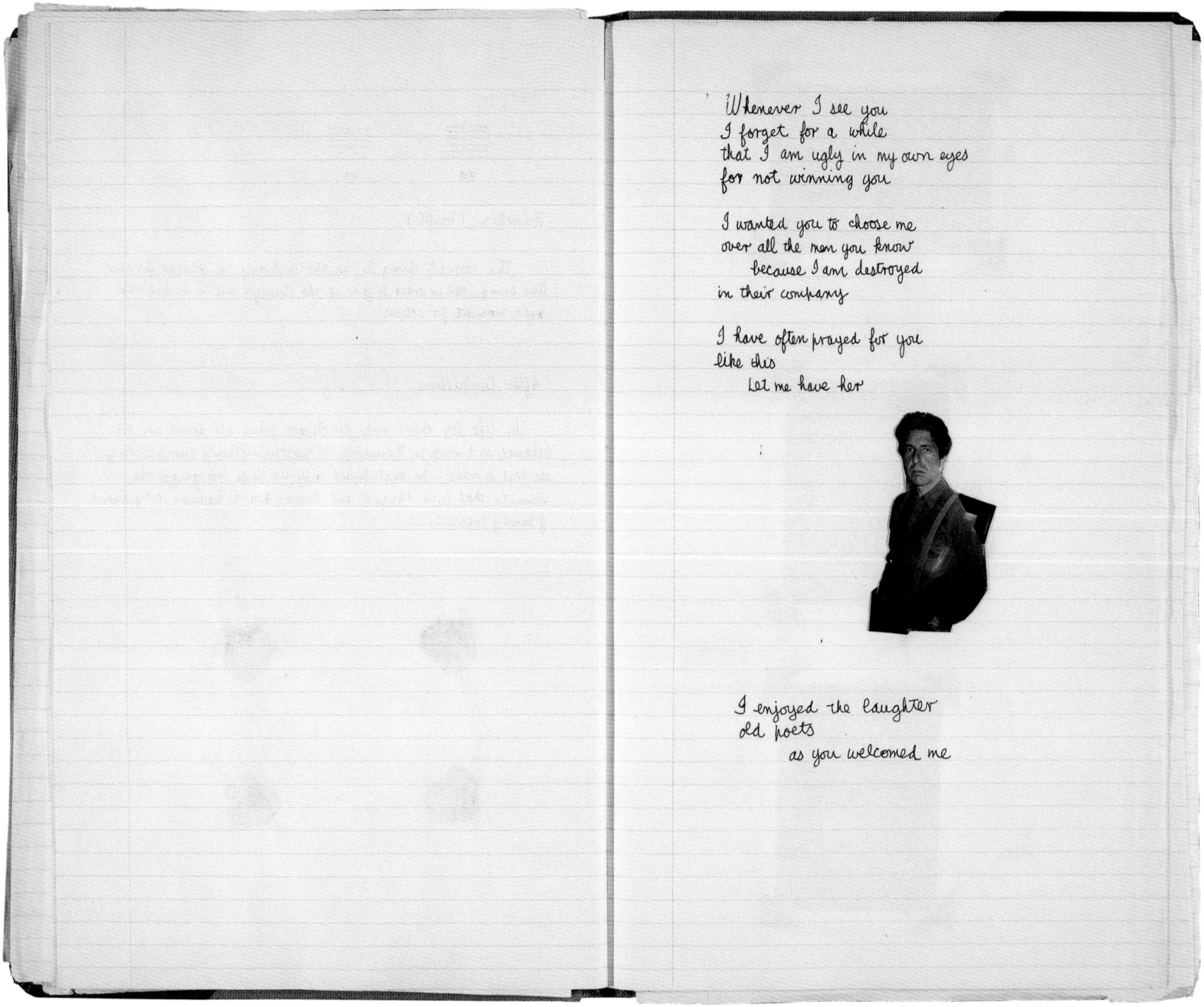

Whenever I see you
I forget for a while
that I am ugly in my own eyes
for not winning you

I wanted you to choose me
over all the men you know
    because I am destroyed
in their company

I have often prayed for you
like this
    Let me have her

I enjoyed the laughter
old poets
        as you welcomed me

Leonard Cohen, *Cohen Cut-Out*, 1968

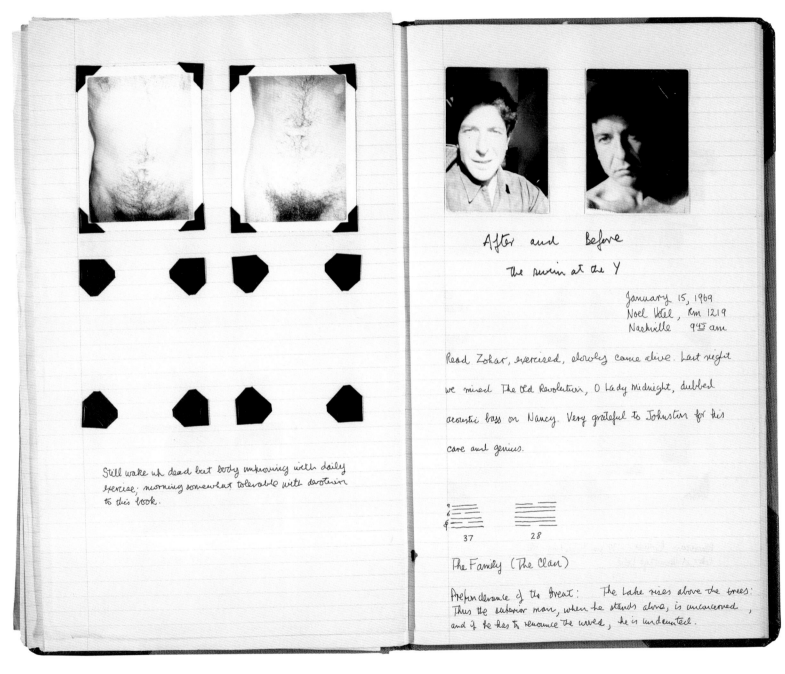

Still wake up dead but body improving with daily exercise; morning somewhat tolerable with devotion to this book.

After and Before
the swim at the Y

January 15, 1969
Noel Hotel, Rm 1219
Nashville 9⁴⁵ am

Read Zohar, exercised, slowly came alive. Last night we mixed The Old Revolution, O Lady Midnight, dubbed acoustic bass on Nancy. Very grateful to Johnston for his care and genius.

37    28

The Family (The Clan)

Preponderance of the Great: The Lake rises above the trees: Thus the superior man, when he stands alone, is unconcerned, and if he has to renounce the world, he is undaunted.

Leonard Cohen, *Nude Torso*, 1968–1969

Leonard Cohen, *After and Before the Swim at the Y*, 1968–1969

"I choose the rooms that I live in with care /
The windows are small, and the walls almost bare."
—Leonard Cohen, "Tonight Will Be Fine,"
from *Songs from a Room* (1968)

In early 1970, Cohen's record label, Columbia, decided to send him on a European tour. Cohen's musical career in Canada and the United States was relatively modest, but in Europe he was already a bit of a cult star, an embodiment of the dark, existential worldview that was prevalent in the culture. The tour was chaotic, to say the least. During his second performance, at the Musikhalle in Hamburg (now the Laeiszhalle), Cohen played a handful of songs, then goose-stepped and addressed the audience with a Sieg Heil, causing much outrage.

At the Isle of Wight Festival on August 26, 1970, Cohen performed after Jimi Hendrix, somehow calming a hostile crowd of 600,000 people who were setting fires, throwing bottles at the stage, and generally causing mayhem. Undaunted, Cohen delivered one of his most celebrated performances. When he and his band—"The Army," as he referred to it—took the stage at 4 am, he called to the crowd: "Can I ask each of you to light a match so I can see where you all are?" According to biographer Sylvie Simmons, "Leonard talked to the hundreds of thousands of people he could not see as if they were sitting together in a small dark room."[5]

Murray Lerner, *Message to Love: The Isle of Wight Festival 1970*, 1970

Cohen's third studio album, *Songs of Love and Hate* was not particularly well received commercially or critically upon its release in the United States and Canada. While the album reached number five on the UK charts, Cohen had been utterly resistant to recording it and had entered a depressive state around this time. Over time, however, the dark, meditative songwriting and production of songs like "Famous Blue Raincoat," "Avalanche," and "Last Year's Man" came to be appreciated and revered as the very definition of "Cohenesque."

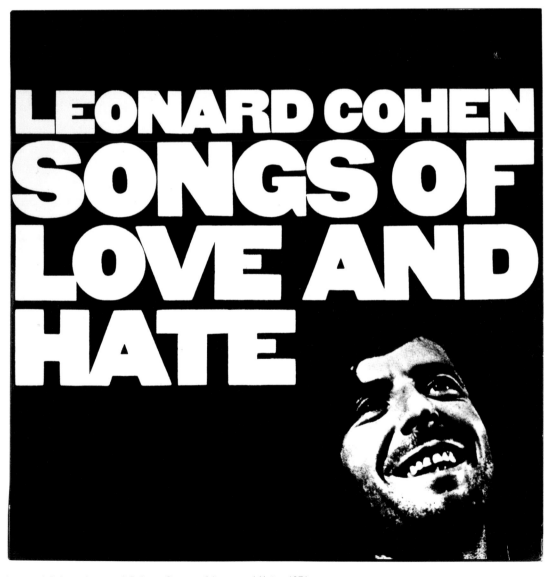

Leonard Cohen, *Leonard Cohen: Songs of Love and Hate,* 1971

Suzanne Elrod, *Acapulco,* 1971

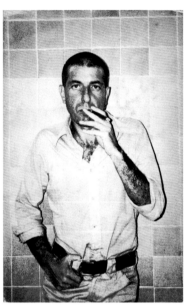

Leonard Cohen, *The Energy of Slaves*
back cover, 1972

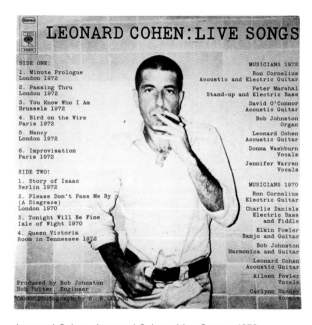

Leonard Cohen, *Leonard Cohen: Live Songs,* 1973

Suzanne Elrod, Cohen's former partner and the mother of his two children, made this photograph of Cohen on a year-end holiday trip to Acapulco. Standing in a tiled bathroom, his hair closely cropped, Cohen brandishes a panatela cigar and looks very much like a rock star. Another photograph from the same occasion was used on the front cover of Cohen's first live album, *Live Songs* (1973), based on recordings from the Isle of Wight concert in 1970 and his subsequent European tour in 1972. The photo was also used for the back cover of *The Energy of Slaves,* Cohen's 1972 book of poetry.

"I've just written a book called *The Energy of Slaves,* and in there I say that I'm in pain. I don't say it in those words because I don't like those words. They don't represent the real situation. It took eighty poems to represent the situation of where I am right now. That to me totally acquits me of any responsibility I have of keeping a public record. I put it in the book. It's carefully worked on. It's taken many years to write and it's there. It'll be between hard covers and it'll be there for as long as people want to keep it in circulation. It's careful and controlled and it's what we call art."[6]

Leonard Cohen, *Self-Portraits,* 1979

Often photographing himself in photo booths or with traditional portable cameras, Cohen enjoyed the process and technology of photography, and over the course of his life owned multiple cameras, including several different models of Polaroid. He photographed himself and those around him intensively. His self-portraits (of which there are hundreds) reveal his ever-present preoccupation with his appearance, which he carefully controlled.

This trio of self-portraits shows Cohen's dual fascination with the creative possibilities of the instant camera and with the photographic exploration of his physical and psychological identity. In all three exposures, Cohen turns the camera on himself, his left arm reaching out of the frame and pointing the instrument back at him. His face carries a questioning, almost suspicious, expression, as if doubting the ability of the camera to capture the particularities of his mood at the time.

This poster was produced as a promotional tool for Cohen's 1972 tour, positioning him for the first time as the "poet of rock music." His signature is visible in the blank orb at the bottom-centre of the composition. Through its typography, colour scheme, and aesthetics, this poster bears many of the hallmarks of rock poster art that became a booming genre in graphic art following the 1967 "Summer of Love."

Unknown maker, *Poet of Rock Music*, 1972

Europe and Israel concert tour footage, 1972

Under pressure from Columbia Records to tour, Cohen assembled a band for a twenty-one-show world tour beginning on March 18, 1972, in Ireland and ending in Israel. These stills are derived from unseen digitized 16mm footage of the 1972 tour.[7] The Leonard Cohen archives contain eleven complete audio concerts of the tour and twenty-two hours of unseen footage.

Unknown photographer, *Leonard Cohen at the Wailing Wall, Jerusalem*, 1973

Recovering on Hydra from his whirlwind world tour and the birth of his first child, Adam, Cohen abruptly left the island and set off for Israel at the outset of the Yom Kippur War. Cohen spent the next twenty days with the Israeli Defense Forces, performing—often several times a day—for troops on the front lines of the conflict between Israel, Egypt, and Syria. He sent this postcard to his sister, Esther, who was then living in New York City, summarizing the situation on the ground in Israel as "Tragic human madness."

Yakovi Doron, *Leonard Performing with Israeli Singer Matti Caspi for Israeli Troops in the Sinai*, 1973

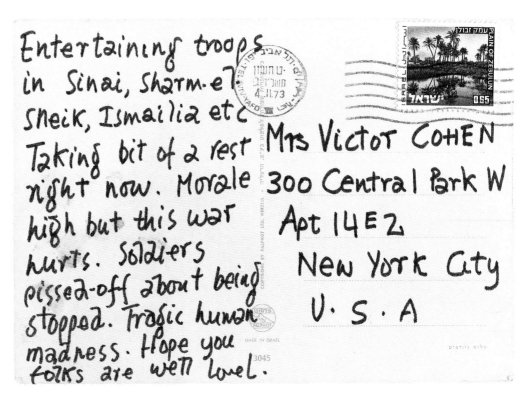

Leonard Cohen, *Postcard to Esther*, 1973

The original cover design for *New Skin for the Old Ceremony* by Teresa Alfiera adapted a 1550 woodcut, the "conjunctio spirituum" from the text *Rosarium philosophorum*, of two naked, winged, and crowned angels in a sexual embrace. The image appears in Carl Jung's *Psychology and Alchemy* (1953), which is quite possibly where Cohen first encountered it, and represents one of Cohen's abiding interests: love in all its dilemmas, manifest in the ideal union of male and female beings which, in alchemy, were embodied in solar and lunar elements respectively.

Columbia Records felt it was too much for the American public. According to Cohen, "A quarter of a million copies have been sold in Europe with this cover and there was not a single reference made to it. Since I designed it, I finally won the battle with Columbia, and they are reinstating the old album cover with a modesty jacket."[8] In fact, for a while, the UK release featured an additional wing covering the genital area of the lovemaking angels, while showing the uncensored image on the back cover. The Korean edition was issued with a monotone green treatment.

Cohen produced this intriguing portrait of himself comingling with a stamped manifestation of the woodcut. The stamp was repurposed for Cohen's book, *Death of a Lady's Man*, in 1978.

Leonard Cohen,
*Self-Portrait Stamped with the Rosarium philosophorum*,
1974

FROM TOP LEFT
(clockwise):

Leonard Cohen,
*New Skin for
the Old Ceremony*,
1974

Leonard Cohen,
*Lover Lover Lover*,
1974

"Fermentatio" in
*Rosarium philosophorum*,
1550

Leonard Cohen,
*Death of Lady's Man*
back cover, 1978

Leonard Cohen,
*Death of Lady's Man*
front cover, 1978

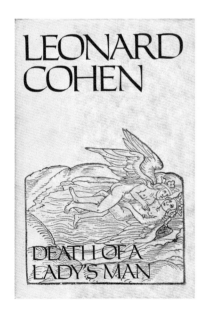

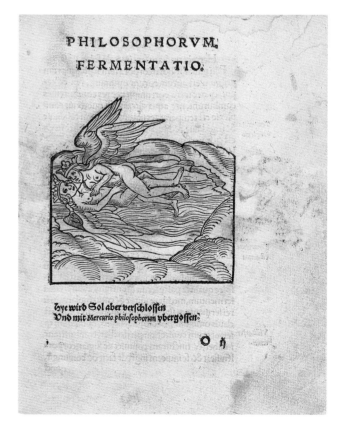

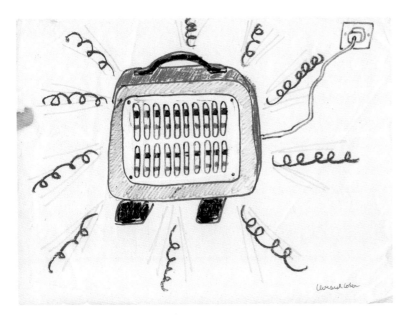

Leonard Cohen, *Hydra Heater*, 1976–1980

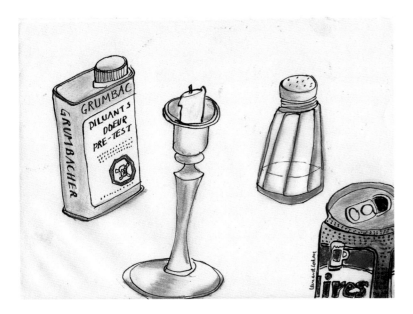

Leonard Cohen, *Still Life*, 1976–1980

Leonard Cohen, *Montreal Still Life (Guitar)*, 1976

In the 1970s, Cohen intensified the daily practice of drawing, using watercolours, pastels, crayons, and other materials at hand, as an extension of his poetry and songwriting. The material shown here demonstrates Cohen's diversity of approaches and the breadth of his creative inclinations.

Leonard Cohen, *Woman with Candlestick,* 1976–1980

Leonard Cohen, *Let Us Be True to One Another,* 1976–1980

Leonard Cohen, *Napkin Sketch,* 1976–1980

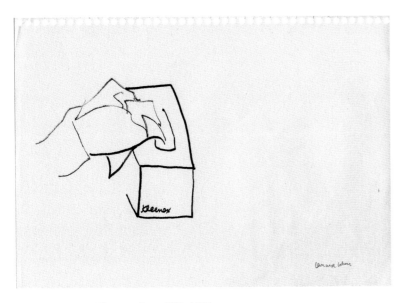

Leonard Cohen, *Kleenex Box,* 1976–1980

## Kleenex Box

Cohen had an uncanny fascination with Kleenex tissues, which are a recurring theme in his first novel, *The Favourite Game* (1963). The book's main protagonist, Lawrence Breavman (understood to be modelled after Cohen's adolescent self), overcomes his insecurity of being almost a head shorter than his friends by stuffing his shoes with Kleenex in order to appear taller for a night out with his date. Throughout the novel, Breavman's relationships, romantic or otherwise, turn out to be temporary and disposable, much like a Kleenex tissue. This quick ink sketch, executed more than a decade later, suggests that Cohen's fixation with the product, and its symbolism, was surprisingly enduring.

Leonard Cohen, *The Room,* 2008–2010

Leonard Cohen, *Salt Shaker,* 1976–1980

Leonard Cohen, *Woman Under Heat Lamp*, 1980–1985

Leonard Cohen, *Lorca's Cup*, 2007

This is the pen I was speaking about
This is the gold pen
This is my favourite grey
This blue is good too
But I prefer a lighter shade

Leonard Cohen, *This Is the Pen I Was Speaking About*, 1976–1980

Lorca's Cup

Cohen took great pleasure in commonplace household objects and paid close attention to them in his domestic surroundings, whether in Montreal, Hydra, Miami, or Los Angeles—places where he spent the most time with his children over the years. This charming drawing of his daughter Lorca's cup has been cut out and collaged onto a blank page in one of Cohen's sketchbooks and is signed by the artist in pencil below the handle.

In the 1980s, Cohen's visual practice became an increasingly integral component of his creative work. He filled many notebooks with drawings executed in various media, including the fourteen watercolours from which these reproductions are excerpted. Each drawing is rendered in a consistent, whimsical style. Some are annotated with a single line or couplet that responds to the content and mood suggested by the drawing. The Dominique referenced in two of the drawings is Dominique Issermann, a French photographer known for her fashion shoots and portraits of writers and artists, from Marguerite Duras to Catherine Deneuve to Leonard Cohen. The two had an eight-year romantic relationship and maintained a close friendship until Cohen's passing. Issermann produced a number of iconic portraits of Cohen, as well as videos for songs such as "First We Take Manhattan" and "Dance Me to the End of Love." Cohen dedicated *I'm Your Man* to Issermann.

Leonard Cohen, *Finally a Solution*, 1980–1985

Leonard Cohen, *Paris Again*, 1980–1985

Leonard Cohen, *Dancers,* 1980–1985

Leonard Cohen, *Self-Portrait,* 1980–1985

Leonard Cohen, *The High Seriousness of Dominique,* 1980–1985

Leonard Cohen, *The Purity of Dominique,* 1980–1985

Leonard Cohen, *Guitar,* 1980–1985

Leonard Cohen, *Woman and Horse,* 1980–1985

In an interview with Robert Enright, Cohen declared that he didn't pretend to understand what was "being asserted so abrasively by so many people in the field of art." He instead went against the grain, and his intention with his visual work "was to make something that was really accessible and that I could decorate my notebooks with."9

Leonard Cohen,
*Portrait of a Woman*
*(Pastel Notebook),*
1980–1985

Leonard Cohen,
*Self-Portrait*
*(Pastel Notebook),*
1980–1985

—

FROM TOP LEFT
(clockwise):

Leonard Cohen,
*Portrait of a Nude Woman*
*(Pastel Notebook),*
1980–1985

Leonard Cohen,
*Portrait of a Nude Woman II*
*(Pastel Notebook),*
1980–1985

Leonard Cohen,
*Portrait of a Nude Woman III*
*(Pastel Notebook),*
1980–1985

Leonard Cohen,
*Self-Portrait II*
*(Pastel Notebook),*
1980–1985

Leonard Cohen,
*Self-Portrait III*
*(Pastel Notebook),*
1980–1985

Leonard Cohen,
*Self-Portrait IV*
*(Pastel Notebook),*
1980–1985

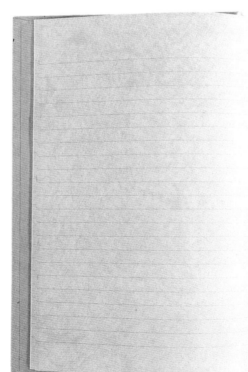

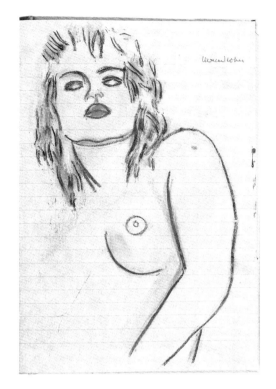

Lynn Ball, *Leonard Cohen on Boulevard Saint-Laurent, Montreal,* c. 1983

Lynn Ball, *Leonard Cohen on Boulevard Saint-Laurent, Montreal*, c. 1983

"I have to keep coming back to Montreal
to renew my neurotic affiliations."
　　—Leonard Cohen

## Adam Cohen

Born Montreal, Quebec, Canada, 1972

The child of Suzanne Elrod and Leonard Cohen, Adam has followed in his father's footsteps as a singer-songwriter in his own right. He spent his early years between Hydra and Montreal as the first of two children, and after his parent's separation in the mid-1970s, Adam and his sister, Lorca, moved to the south of France with their mother. Picking up music as a young boy, Adam taught himself drums, guitar, and piano by the age of twelve. As a recording artist, he has released four major albums, three of them in English and one in French. Working closely with his father, Adam produced and performed on Leonard's 2016 album, *You Want It Darker*, and compiled and produced the posthumous album of Leonard's music, *Thanks for the Dance*.

## Lorca Cohen

Born Montreal, Quebec, Canada, 1974

Lorca Cohen, named after Leonard's favourite poet, Federico García Lorca, is the second child of Suzanne Elrod and Leonard Cohen. Born two years after her brother, Adam, Lorca spent her early childhood in Hydra and Montreal. She attended school in Paris after her mother relocated her and Adam to the south of France, and afterward, boarding school in Vermont. Lorca's photography was featured in many of the tour books and other merchandise for her father's 2008–2010 tour. In 2010, she co-curated with Darrin Klein a film composition featuring interpretations of the songs on *New Skin for the Old Ceremony*. The film was shown at the Hammer Museum and The Museum of Modern Art.

Unknown photographer, *Adam Cohen*, c. 1975

Unknown photographer, *Lorca Cohen*, c. 1980

Leonard Cohen, *Lorca,
Leonard, and Adam Cohen
Photo Booth Strip*, 1978

Unknown photographer, *Cohen at Home in Montreal*, 1975–1980

## Suzanne Elrod
Born Miami, Florida, United States, 1950

Suzanne Elrod is the mother of Leonard Cohen's two children, Adam and Lorca. Suzanne and Leonard met in the spring of 1969 while attending classes at the Scientology Centre in New York. They quickly became involved; Suzanne left her partner to move into Leonard's room in the Chelsea Hotel, while also spending time at a ranch in Franklin, Tennessee, that Cohen tried to make his home. By all accounts, they had a rocky relationship and were emotionally volatile and sexually competitive. Nevertheless, in 1972, Adam was born in Montreal, followed two years later by Lorca in 1974. By the late '70s, the relationship had deteriorated so significantly that the couple separated. Although they were never legally married, they finalized a divorce settlement in 1979 arranged by Steve Machat. Suzanne then moved to the south of France with Adam and Lorca.

Unknown photographer, *Adam Cohen,
Suzanne Elrod, Leonard Cohen, and Masha Cohen
in Montreal*, 1972

After spending most of the 1960s between Hydra and New York, Cohen returned to Montreal in the 1970s and purchased a home in the Saint-Laurent neighbourhood, near the city's tiny Parc du Portugal. Cohen and Suzanne Elrod made Montreal their home for a while, and their children, Adam and Lorca, were born there in 1972 and 1974 respectively. Cohen's creative output continued to be adventurous and prodigious: he recorded and released *Death of a Ladies' Man* (1977) and *Recent Songs* (1979); released the book *Death of a Lady's Man* (1978); embarked on the *Field Commander Cohen* tour in Europe (1979) with Jennifer Warnes and, for the first time,

Sharon Robinson, as well as Roshi, his Zen Buddhist teacher; collaborated with photographers and playwrights on various projects; and worked with producer Harry Rasky on *The Song of Leonard Cohen*, a feature-length special for the CBC (1980). At the same time, Cohen continued travelling to Los Angeles for various recording projects, and to be near Roshi's Zen Center on Mt. Baldy. Cohen retreated from the limelight in the early 1980s, travelling between Mt. Baldy, Montreal, Hydra, and France. In 1983, he wrote and starred in the short experimental video musical *I Am a Hotel*.

Unknown photographer, *Leonard Cohen*, c. 1979

Leonard Cohen, *I Am a Hotel*, 1983

Leonard Cohen, *Greatest Hits,* 1975

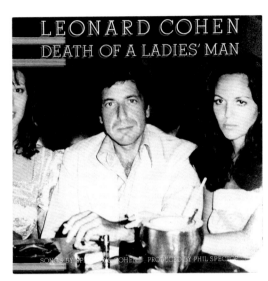

Leonard Cohen, *Death of a Ladies' Man,* 1977

Leonard Cohen, *Field Commander Cohen:*
*Tour of 1979,* 2001

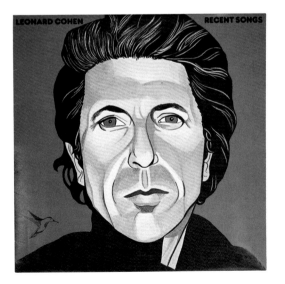

Leonard Cohen, *Recent Songs,* 1979

Leonard Cohen's fifth studio album was released in November 1977 to generally poor reviews. Cohen himself said the songs were good but that the production by Phil Spector was terrible, especially as it reduced Cohen's vocals to another brick in the famous wall of sound. One wonders what the introverted, understated Cohen expected from the master of bombastic rock 'n' roll music. In the end, it sounds very much like a Spector record, but is also unmistakably a Cohen record, with his reflections on falling in and out of love, on betrayal, denial, and vengeance, coming through loud and clear. Cohen's partnership with Suzanne Elrod was falling apart as he wrote this album and the book that followed, as evidenced in lyrics from songs like "Paper-Thin Hotel": "A heavy burden lifted from my soul / I learned that love was out of my control / I felt so good I couldn't feel a thing."

Ira Nadel remarked about Cohen's book *Death of a Lady's Man*: "Its 216 pages mix poetry with journal entries expressing the lyrical, dramatic, and musical. Persistent themes such as sexual self-pity, betrayal, and masochistic revelation shape the text. The violation of solemn contracts—expressed through self-deprecation and mystical invocation, the use of magic and religious ceremony... creates an absorbing book that is something of a summa of Cohen's life to 1977. Suddenly, popular culture and the apocalypse had united."[10]

Unknown photographer, *Leonard Cohen in Montreal*, c. 1975

Unknown photographer, *Leonard Cohen in Hydra*, c. 1974

Harry Rasky, *The Song of Leonard Cohen*, 1980

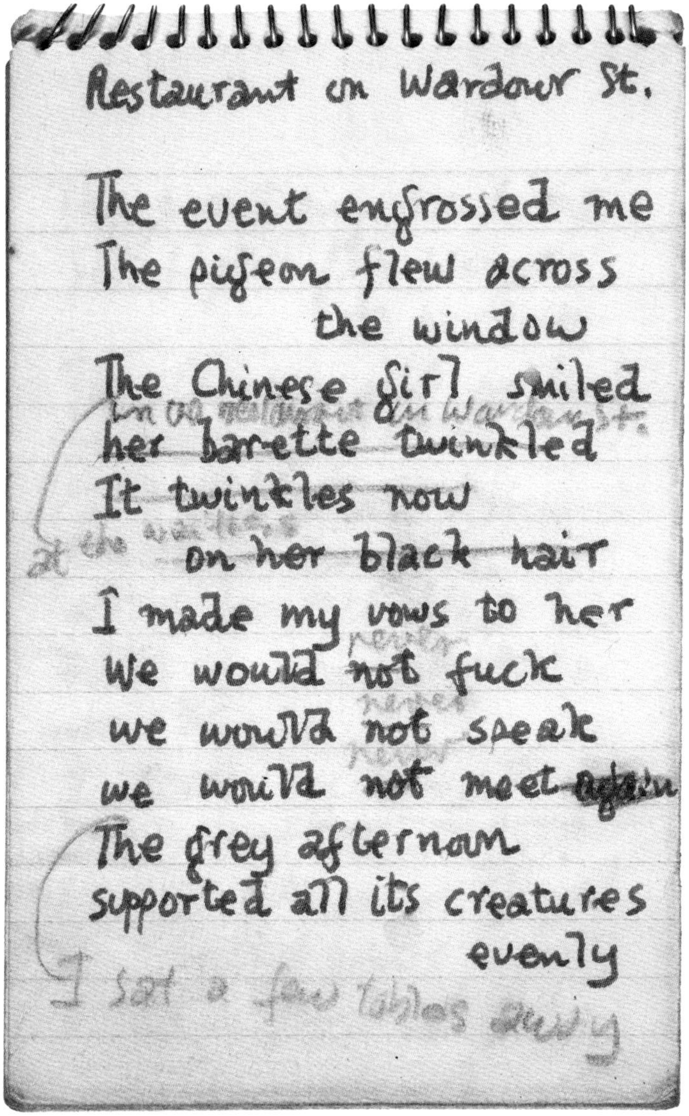

Restaurant on Wardour St.

The event engrossed me
The pigeon flew across
            the window
The Chinese girl smiled
her barrette twinkled
It twinkles now
            on her black hair
I made my vows to her
we would not fuck
we would not speak
we would not meet again
The grey afternoon
supported all its creatures
                    evenly
I sat a few tables away

She loved his open window
    & she loved his royal view
She loved the sparrow in his hand
    that he was listening to
She beckoned & the reeling
    of his high religious mood
She made a space between her legs
    she took his solitude

He stood before a window
like a captain master of his view
She held the sparrow in his hand
that heaven listens to
She beckoned to the reeling
of his high religious mood
She made a space between her legs
    she took his solitude

Leonard Cohen, "The Event" (*1972 Notebook*),
published in *Death of a Lady's Man*, 1978

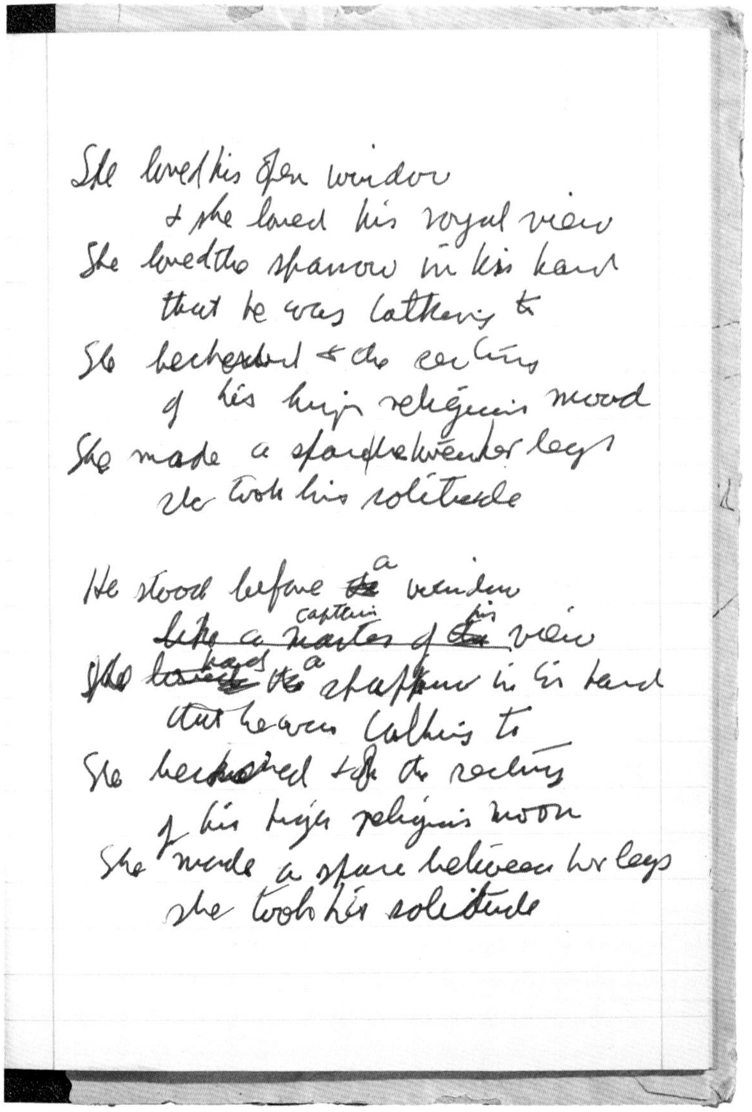

Leonard Cohen, "Death of a Lady's Man" (*1973 Hydra Notebook*),
published in *Death of a Lady's Man*, 1978

Lynn Ball, *Contact Sheet*, c. 1985

Leonard Cohen, *Self-Portrait: Various Positions, Outtake 1*, 1984

Leonard Cohen, *Self-Portrait: Various Positions, Outtake 2*, 1984

Leonard Cohen, *Self-Portrait: Various Positions, Outtake 3*, 1984

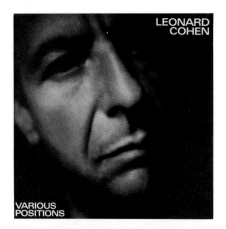

Leonard Cohen,
*Various Positions*, 1984

With songs like "Dance Me to the End of Love," "A Singer Must Die," and "Heart with No Companion," Cohen and his producer John Lissauer were certain that *Various Positions* was his best record to date. Walter Yetnikoff, then studio head of Columbia Records, disagreed and refused to give the record a mainstream US release. Instead, the album was quietly released in the United States via the small, independent label Passport Records, and basically disappeared. Many years later, as "Hallelujah" became an essential part of 21st-century culture, *Various Positions* (1984) found its audience and Cohen and Lissauer were vindicated.

One of Cohen's most iconic songs, "Hallelujah" took him almost five years to complete, and finally found a place on the album *Various Positions*. Cohen wrote multiple versions—the lore is that he experimented with more than 150 verses—and it was years before he settled on the final lyrics. The song shows Cohen's embrace of biblical imagery, and his gift for combining the sacred and the profane.

"Hallelujah," words and music by Leonard Cohen, 1979–1984

Richard McCaffrey, *Leonard Cohen and Jennifer Warnes with Sharon Robinson and Mitch Watkins perform live at the Greek Theatre in Berkeley, California*, 1983

## Jennifer Warnes
Born Seattle, Washington, United States, 1947

Jennifer Warnes is a two-time Grammy-winning musician and producer. Moving into folk music in her early twenties, she was signed by Parrot Records in 1968. Warnes auditioned for Cohen's producer Bob Johnston in preparation for the 1972 world tour, and subsequently developed a life-long relationship with Cohen. Initially signed as a backup singer, she later worked as vocal arranger on subsequent tours and albums. In 1986,

Warnes recorded a compilation of covers of Cohen's music under the title *Famous Blue Raincoat*. Cohen and the production team reworked several songs with Warnes, and helped with the making of her music video "First We Take Manhattan." *Famous Blue Raincoat* was a huge critical and commercial success, and set the stage for the release of Cohen's *I'm Your Man*.

Jennifer Warnes,
*Famous Blue Raincoat,* 1986

Cohen developed many close professional relationships with women during his career, including American singer-songwriter Jennifer Warnes. Warnes wrote "The Song of Bernadette" while on Cohen's 1979 tour, the initial lyrics about a conversation between herself and the child she might have been; the song later developed into one of many collaborative projects with Cohen. "The Song of Bernadette" appeared on Warnes's 1986 tribute album, *Famous Blue Raincoat*—the only song on the album that Cohen himself never recorded.

Leonard Cohen, "There Was a Child Named Bernadette," 1986

Leonard Cohen, "There Was a Child Named Bernadette II," 1986

## I'm Your Man, 1987

*I'm Your Man* was greeted by critics and the public alike as a come-back, establishing a "new Cohen." The featured synth keyboards, drum machines, and other electronic instruments became his signature sound throughout subsequent decades, coupled with the gravelly voice that also became trademark Cohen. The album contains many of Cohen's most popular songs, including "First We Take Manhattan," which initially appeared on Jennifer Warnes's *Famous Blue Raincoat* LP; the Federico García Lorca-inspired "Take This Waltz"; and "Everybody Knows," a song Cohen co-wrote with Sandra Robinson. Jason Ankeny wrote that it was a "stunningly sophisticated leap into modern musical textures [and that] *I'm Your Man* re-establishes Leonard Cohen's mastery. Against a backdrop of keyboards and propulsive rhythms, Cohen surveys the global landscape with a precise, unflinching eye: the opening 'First We Take Manhattan' is an ominous fantasy of commercial success bundled in crypto-fascist imagery, while the remarkable 'Everybody Knows' is a cynical catalog of the land mines littering the surface of love in the age of AIDS."[11]

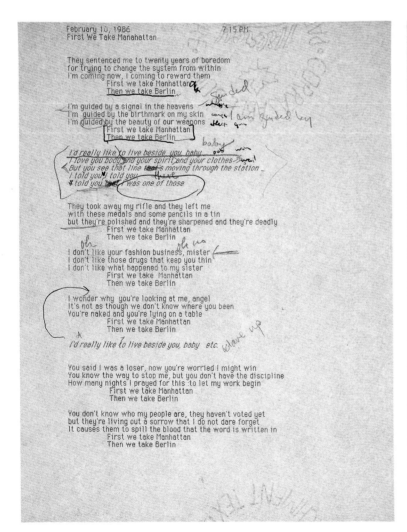

Leonard Cohen, "First We Take Manhattan," 1986

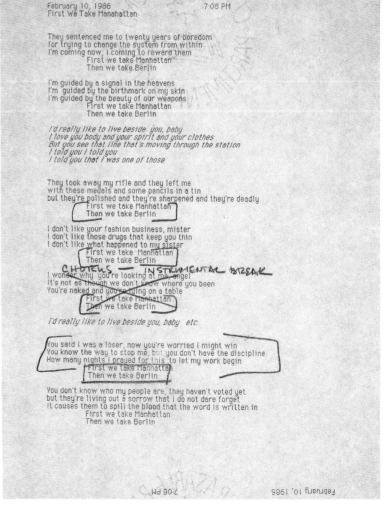

Leonard Cohen, "First We Take Manhattan II," 1986

In the 1980s, the synthesizer—a desktop-sized electronic keyboard in its most common form—became a mainstay instrument in popular music and featured prominently in Cohen's 1988 album, *I'm Your Man*. At the touch of a button, the user could access a variety of standard rhythms, from the waltz and foxtrot to rock, polka, and reggae. Cohen took to using a synthesizer as much as his guitar to explore musical ideas, once remarking: "With all these advantages, it makes the instrument very lovable."[12]

This song sheet—which features the lyrics and music for "Everybody Knows" written in rich cursive—was created for the recording studio and for rehearsals, and designed in a way that it could be unfolded on a music stand as needed. Cohen was meticulous in his preparations for live performance and put his band through lengthy rehearsals prior to embarking on his international tours.

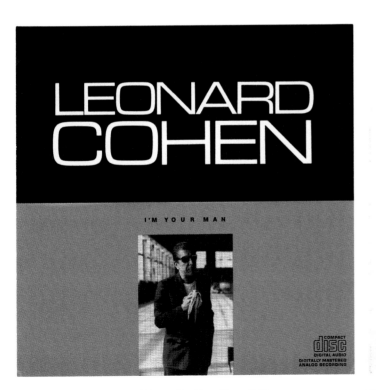

Leonard Cohen, *Leonard Cohen: I'm Your Man*, 1988

"Everybody Knows," words and music by Leonard Cohen and Sharon Robinson, 1988

Dear Leonard,
          You have ruined my life for me
by teaching me not only to aim for perfection but to
achieve it. How can I go on as before after tasting
the _very best_? I feel the only fitting end to such
a night would be to fling myself under a truck
on the harbour bridge, like Vivien Leigh once
did in the London fog! Did you see that movie?
My beautiful Leonard, believe that I love you
and that we could've taught each other many
things. I'm not sure I should have left
you sleeping after all — I should have

Unknown author, Fan mail, 1979

...the Dreamer
ride against
the Men of Action,
oh see
the Men of
Action
falling back...

For Leonard, in Vienna, in a smoke-dried
studio, trying to put his songs into the
very best German — with an old tape-
recorder and the voice after 100
cigarettes, but nonetheless with
undefeatable energy & love,
Espen
March, 9, 1980

Unknown author, Fan mail with drawing, 1980

Leonard Cohen's music has been covered ever since Judy Collins included some cuts on her 1966 LP, *In My Life*. In 1991, many heavy hitters in the indie music scene contributed songs to *I'm Your Fan: The Songs of Leonard Cohen*. Among other highlights, the album included John Cale's cover of "Hallelujah," a recut of Cohen's original and the version that found its way onto the *Shrek* soundtrack, eventually inspiring Jeff Buckley's iconic recording. To date, there are at least 3,500 recorded covers of Cohen's songs, including

Joan Baez, *Letter from Joan*, 1994

Joni Mitchell, *Telegram from Joni*, 1970

Joni Mitchell, *Telegram from Joni II*, 1970

800 of "Hallelujah," alone. Cohen's fanbase is massive and diverse, and includes music enthusiasts and lovers of literature, as well as fellow giants of popular music such as Nick Cave, Beck, Iggy Pop, Bono and U2, Elton John, and Bob Dylan. Cohen received massive amounts of correspondence from fans and acquaintances throughout his career.

Various artists,
*I'm Your Fan: The Songs of Leonard Cohen*, 1991

Unknown photographer, *Leonard Cohen and Elton John*, c. 1993

Beck, *Songs of Leonard Cohen*, 2017

Unknown photographer,
*Leonard Cohen and U2*, 2001

Don Was, *Leonard Cohen and Iggy Pop*, 1989

k.d. lang

leonard.

my profound thanks...
for your kind words at
the junos.
i am forever grateful
and indebted to you for
writing such anthems to
humanity.  my best to you.

Suite #412 | 3940 Laurel Canyon Boulevard | Studio City California 91604

k.d. lang, *Note to Cohen*, 2013

After a well-received tour in support of *I'm Your Man*, Cohen took a year off to be with his son, Adam, who was recovering from a car accident that left him in a coma for four months. In Sylvie Simmons's *I'm Your Man: The Life of Leonard Cohen*, actor Rebecca De Mornay recounts a conversation with Cohen about why he wanted to live in Los Angeles: "'You have a place in beautiful Montreal, and Hydra, and you've lived in New York and Paris. Why here?' Leonard replied, 'This is the place. It's like a metaphor of the decline. The whole system is coming apart. I can feel it. The future is grim, and Los Angeles is at the centre of it. It has the decay and some sort of wile hope too, like weeds growing through the asphalt. I want to write from this place, from what's really going on.' De Mornay responded, 'Wow, okay, we're living in the decay, you at the bottom and me at the top of this one street. Great.' And from within that he wrote *The Future*."[13] The album embraces a variety of musical forms, from gospel choruses and country to marching-band rhythms and synthpop—or, at least, Cohen's take on each of them.

Leonard Cohen, *The Future*, 1992

91

the graceful trees of Hollywood
swayed outside my window
I would have liked to help you
but my hands were tied
in my fortieth year
I finally knew
beauty at close quarter
+ how it changed the room
+ made men pull their stomachs in
and down
I mean that I was living in a swivel
all this up with the beauty of Rebecca

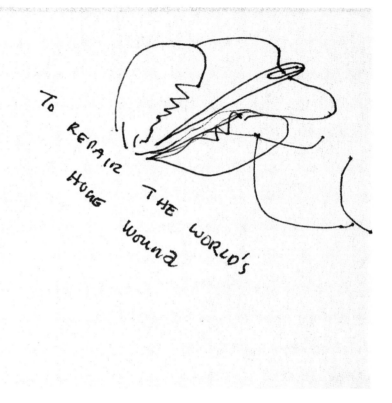

To Repair the World's Huge Wound

Leonard Cohen, *To Repair the World's Huge Wound*, c. 1990

## Rebecca De Mornay
Born Santa Rosa, California, United States, 1959

Rebecca De Mornay is an American actress who rose to prominence in the 1980s with her breakout role opposite Tom Cruise in *Risky Business*. Cohen and De Mornay met on a number of occasions in the mid-'80s before solidifying a friendship in 1987, which later became a romantic partnership and the pair ultimately getting engaged. De Mornay and Cohen developed a close working relationship during this time, and she is credited as a co-producer on his 1992 LP *The Future,* which was also dedicated to her. In 1993, the couple ended their engagement.

Leonard Cohen, *Rebecca De Mornay*, c. 1992

Cohen first drafted the song "Democracy" as the Soviet Union was collapsing (1988–1991) and the spread of democratic ideals was taking shape in eastern Europe. The song took shape as a subtle and biting critique of the experiment of democracy in the United States. Cohen's lyrics paint a somewhat bleak picture of the future, deftly blending world events to examine rhetoric, religion, politics, and the spread of fundamentalist ideology across the globe.

## DEMOCRACY

It's coming through a hole in the air;
from those nights in Tienenman Square.
It's coming from the feel
that it ain't exactly real,
or it's real, but it ain't exactly there.
From the wars against disorder,
from the sirens night and day;
from the fires of the homeless,
from the ashes of the gay:
Democracy is coming to the U.S.A.

It's coming through a crack in the wall;
on a visionary flood of alcohol;
from the staggering account
of the Sermon on the Mount
which I don't pretend to understand at all.
It's coming from the silence
on the dock of the bay,
from the brave, the bold, the battered heart
of Chevrolet:
Democracy is coming to the U.S.A.

It's coming from the sorrow on the street;
the holy places where the races meet;
from the homicidal bitching
that goes down in every kitchen
to determine who will serve and who will eat.
From the wells of disappointment
where the women kneel to pray
for the Grace of G-d in the desert here
and the desert far away:
Democracy is coming to the U.S.A.

*Sail on, sail on*
*O mighty Ship of State!*
*To the Shores of Need*
*Past the Reefs of Greed*
*Through the Squalls of Hate*
*Sail on, sail on, sail on...*

I'm sentimental, if you know what I mean:
I love the country but I can't stand the scene.
And I'm neither left or right,
I'm just staying home tonight,
getting lost in that hopeless little screen.
But I'm stubborn as those garbage bags
that Time cannot decay,
I'm junk but I'm still holding up
this little wild bouquet:
Democracy is coming to the U.S.A.

*Sail on, sail on*
*O mighty Ship of State!*
*To the Shores of Need*
*Past the Reefs of Greed*
*Through the Squalls of Hate*
*Sail on, sail on, sail on...*

It's coming to America first,
the cradle of the best and of the worst.
It's here they got the range
and the machinery for change
and it's here they got the spiritual thirst.
It's here the family's broken
and it's here the lonely say
that the heart has got to open
in a fundamental way:
Democracy is coming to the U.S.A.

It's coming from the women and the men.
O baby, we'll be making love again.
We'll be going down so deep
that the river's going to weep,
and the mountain's going to shout Amen!
It's coming like the tidal flood
beneath the lunar sway,
imperial, mysterious,
in array:
Democracy is coming to the U.S.A.

FROM TOP LEFT
(clockwise):

Leonard Cohen,
"Democracy Is Coming
to the USA," 1992

Leonard Cohen,
"Democracy Is Coming
to the USA" (page 1),
1992

Leonard Cohen,
"Democracy Is Coming
to the USA" (page 2),
1992

Leonard Cohen,
"Democracy Is Coming
to the USA" (page 3),
1992

Sound the bells that still can sound
Gather all good men around
Say they stand on holy ground
If you can speak at all
              talk

The wars they will be fought again
The heart led out to walk again
You may see me falter there
You may see me fall

Ring the bells that still can ring
Forget your perfect offering
There is a crack in everything
And everything's a wall

                    I know you don't believe in me
I can get them for you, I can get them free
        ✗ I can get me for you free
    I can get them for you free

We're broken almost perfectly
We're not even two

The nausea of men absent
the birth delayed, the marriage spent
the widowhood of government
She's naked but there isn't much to see
and you're not even broken perfectly

Leonard Cohen,

Unknown photographer, *Cohen at Mt. Baldy, California*, November 5, 1995

Leonard Cohen was a spiritual seeker throughout his adult life. Always true to his Jewish roots, he was engaged with Christianity, Scientology (briefly), and different forms of meditation. In 1973, he met Joshu Sasaki Roshi, a Japanese Zen Buddhist monk, and began practising the most sustained aspect of his spirituality. He bought a house near Roshi's Mt. Baldy Zen Center in the San Gabriel mountains east of Los Angeles in 1978. Shortly after completing his 1993 world tour and his breakup from fiancée Rebecca De Mornay, Cohen committed himself to the life of a monk and under the tutelage of master Roshi, he spent the following five years practising Buddhism at the Zen Center. In 1996, Cohen was ordained as a Zen monk and given a new name: Jikan.

As this photograph shows, Cohen sat meditating in half lotus—for many hours a day. In 1998, Cohen found himself deeply depressed and made the difficult decision to leave Mt. Baldy, travelling to Mumbai to study with an Advaita Hindu teacher named Ramesh S. Balsekar. "Something had happened to Leonard in India. Something—as he told [songwriter] Sharon Robinson—'just lifted' the veil of depression through which he had always seen the world. Over the space of several visits Leonard would make to Mumbai over the next few years . . . he spent more than a year studying with Ramesh. . . . 'By imperceptible degrees this background of anguish that had been with me my whole life began to dissolve. I said to myself [that] this must be what it's like to be relatively sane.' His depression was gone."[14]

Dear Roshi,
I'm sorry that I cannot
help you now, because
I met this woman.

Please forgive my
selfishness.

I send you
Birthday Greetings
deep affection and
respect.

Jikan
the useless monk
bows his head

Leonard Cohen, *Dear Roshi*, c. 1998

no Roshi
no Guru
no Rebbe

I lift my glass
to Mt Baldy

Jikan
who pretended
to be a monk
bows his head

Leonard Cohen, *Salute to Roshi*, 1999

## Joshu Sasaki Roshi

Born Miyagi Prefecture, Japan, 1907
Died Los Angeles, California, United States, 2014

Joshu Sasaki Roshi was a Zen Buddhist monk and abbot of the Mt. Baldy Zen Center, a retreat that played a central role in Cohen's exploration of Buddhism. Sasaki began his training at the age of fourteen under the tutelage of Joten Soko Miura Roshi, a master in the Rinzai school of Zen Buddhism. By the age of forty, Sasaki had risen to the rank of Roshi, taking over care of Shoju-an, a remote monastery in the Japanese Alps founded by Shoju Ronin, teacher of the great eighteenth-century Zen master Hakuin. In 1962, Sasaki relocated to the United States, setting up two training centres: one near Los Angeles (Mt. Baldy) and the other in Albuquerque (Bodhi Manda). The Mt. Baldy Zen Center featured heavily in Cohen's life and poetry, and resulted in his very close relationship with the Zen master. Today, Roshi is remembered as the last of a generation of pioneering Japanese Zen monks.

Don Farber, *Leonard and Roshi*, c. 1996

Leonard Cohen, *Angry at 11 pm,* 1991

Leonard Cohen, *Bottles and Candles,* 1991

Leonard Cohen, *Cow Butter Dish, Salt & Pepper,* 1991

Leonard Cohen, *Cup,* 1991

Leonard Cohen, *Self-Portrait,* 2000

Leonard Cohen, *Guitar and Key,* 1993

Leonard Cohen, *Self-Portrait,* 1984

*Ten New Songs* was Cohen's tenth album and his first album in a decade. When he left Mt. Baldy, he had written over 250 songs. Cohen asked Sharon Robinson to write the melodies, and the result was a full-blown collaboration, with Robinson writing, arranging, producing, and singing on the album. The venerable rock critic Anthony DeCurtis wrote that "*Songs* is aided by Robinson's atmospheric synths and muted hip-hop rhythms, which respectively envelop and lift Cohen's low-pitched whisperings as he addresses fantasy ('In My Secret Life'), regret ('Alexandra Leaving'), and hope ('The Land of Plenty'). At 67, Cohen is simply a master practicing his craft, and while *Ten New Songs* is not an attempt to break new ground, its sophistication and unassuming depth are almost worth the decade-long wait."[15]

Leonard Cohen, *Ten New Songs,* 2001

## Sharon Robinson

Born San Francisco, California, United States, 1958

Sharon Robinson is an American musician and producer, and was a frequent collaborator with Cohen. She first joined Cohen's 1979 world tour as a backup singer alongside Jennifer Warnes, which began her lifelong friendship with Cohen; he went on to act as godfather to Robinson's son. The pair wrote "Everybody Knows" together in the late 1980s, and in 2001 she co-wrote and produced *Ten New Songs*, Cohen's first album in ten years. Robinson also sang, arranged choirs, and played synth bass on Cohen's 2002 *Dear Heather* LP, and her 2008 LP, *Everybody Knows*, features three Cohen covers. She rejoined Cohen in 2008 as he re-emerged from a long hiatus and performed alongside him on his most successful tours through 2013.

Ethan Hill, *Sharon Robinson and Leonard Cohen*, 2001

Over the course of his long career, Cohen played hundreds of concerts all over the world—but performing for crowds did not become second nature until he was in his seventies. In 2007, he conceived a world tour with a full band—his first in fifteen years—including three backup singers, two guitarists, a drummer, keyboardist, bassist, and saxophonist (later replaced by a violinist). He rehearsed with the band rigorously for three months prior to the start of the tour in Halifax, Nova Scotia, and travelled all over the globe during the next five years, from New York to Nice, Moscow to Sydney. Cohen gave it his all, several nights a week, and 380 shows in packed arenas later, the tour ended in Auckland in late December 2013.

Sharon Robinson would quip about the length of the shows, which sometimes lasted as long as four hours. These concerts were critically acclaimed and brought him considerable personal and creative satisfaction.

Leonard Cohen, *Keyboard and Minora,* 2009

In September 2009, Cohen performed at Tel Aviv's Ramat Gan Stadium, his first performance in Israel since 1985. The concert was controversial, set against the recent cessation of hostilities between Palestine and the Israeli Defense Forces during the Gaza–Israel conflict. Cohen dedicated the concert to the cause of "reconciliation, tolerance, and peace," and the song "Anthem" to the bereaved, donating the proceeds to Israel-Palestinian peace organizations. At the end of the concert, Cohen raised his hands, rabbinically, and recited in Hebrew the *birkat kohanim*—the Priestly Blessing—to the crowd.

Unknown videographer, *Live in Tel Aviv*, 2009

Leonard Cohen, *Old Ideas World Tour* newspaper ad, 2012

Leonard Cohen, *Old Ideas,* 2012

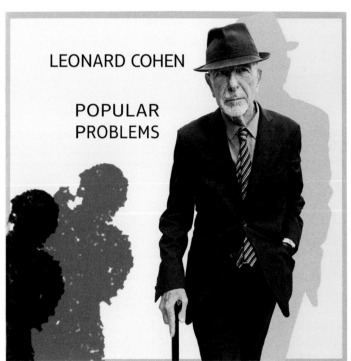

Leonard Cohen, *Popular Problems,* 2014

Seven years after his last recording at age seventy-seven, and after his triumphant world tour, Cohen released an album that continued his musical adventurousness. *Old Ideas* (2012) moved away from his synthesizer-driven approach and embraced a more eclectic interplay of country, gypsy jazz, and blues. The album marked an intense and productive relationship with songwriter, musician, and producer Patrick Leonard, best known for his collaborations with Madonna, and also reached No. 3 on the Billboard 200 Albums Chart. This was the highest ever for a Cohen record, and the first to top the Canadian Albums Chart, a feat he repeated with his follow-up, *Popular Problems* (2014), which was largely co-written and produced by Patrick Leonard.

Kezban Ozcan, *Leonard Cohen and Patrick Leonard*, c. 2013

## Anjani Thomas
Born Honolulu, Hawaii, United States, 1959

Anjani Thomas is an American singer-songwriter and one of Cohen's former partners. She performed on Cohen's original 1984 recording of "Hallelujah" and accompanied him on his 1985 tour as a keyboardist and backup vocalist, in addition to working on his later albums *I'm Your Man*, *The Future*, *Dear Heather*, and *Old Ideas*. Thomas also had a solo career under her first name, releasing *Anjani* in 2000 and *The Sacred Names* in 2001. In this photo she stands in front of an icon of Kateri Tekakwitha, a 17th-century Algonquin-Mohawk woman who was shunned by her community for her religious conversion to Catholicism and is now venerated as a patron saint of ecology.

Leonard Cohen, *Anjani*, 2000

Leonard Cohen's Unified Heart first appears on the cover
of *Book of Mercy* (1984). The symbol is derived from
the Star of David but was intended to transcend religions,
philosophies, and ideologies. Cohen has described it
as "a version of the yin and yang or any of those symbols
that incorporate the polarities . . . and try and reconcile
the differences."[16]

# ESSAYS

*Leonard Cohen: The Future World Tour* leather jacket, 1993

# ACCEPTABLE DECORATIONS

## A CONVERSATION WITH MICHAEL PETIT

Julian Cox

**Julian Cox:** Can you tell me a little about your background and education?

**Michael Petit:** I came out to California to go to college and eventually ended up at UCLA, majoring in literature and fine art. I graduated and wanted to get into animation, but the early 1970s was an awful time for animation, so I ended up doing graphic design at my own studio. I worked for an ad agency and did a lot of freelance stuff; I went back to working with my own clients starting in 1984, and then full-time in 1991. Mostly high-end print production, entertainment industry ads, the usual gambit of graphic design things: corporate identity, logos, brochures, a lot of print production trade journals. And that's basically me.

JC: How did you meet Leonard Cohen? Was it through a direct connection with your profession?

MP: I was doing my own projects and also freelancing for other people, including a printer in Glendale that got an inquiry from Leonard's company Stranger Management—Stranger Music, then—about an engraved invitation that they did for a Spanish embassy function. They wanted something similar. I took the meeting, and that was the first thing I produced: an engraved, embossed invitation, map, and silk banners for a dinner in honour of Roshi's [Cohen's teacher and Zen master's] eighty-fifth birthday. And part of that was to develop Roshi's logo as a cloisonné pin. Leonard was a big fan of cloisonné at that point, too.

Fig. 1 Leonard Cohen, *Cohen's Desk* (Los Angeles), 1991

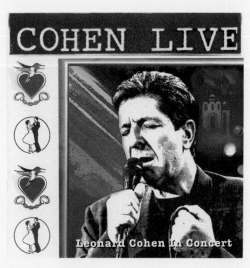

Fig. 2 Leonard Cohen, *Cohen Live,* 1994

This was 1992. And when that happened, Leonard said, "Oh, well, you know, we're about to do a tour, and we could use some stuff." And so, I made merchandise for what was *The Future* tour, which consisted of the tour book, a beautiful leather jacket with an embroidery patch.... We had mugs and, of course, *The Future* cloisonné pin, and a variety of things. The temporary tattoos were a fun extra, and there was also *The Future* watch, among other merch and swag (see pages 115–117). I think Lorca Cohen or maybe Kelley Lynch got a whole set of china with the logo made. I did all this after working with Leonard on the concept art for the album—the symbol of the heart and the hummingbird and handcuffs, which was very meaningful for him at the time. I asked him about it, and, you know, poets don't particularly like to share interpretations of their work, but he spoke about it as an ongoing struggle for dominance in the human heart, between the freedom impulse represented by the hummingbird and the restraint and control and the darker side represented by the cuff, the manacles.

JC: Can you describe how you collaborated with Cohen?

MP: Well, he had ideas, and I had a print production background. Rather than just being an art director/concept guy, I was always trying to be hands-on and do the production myself, so that I was familiar with the process and the requirements of print reproduction. Tools were changing then, dramatically. For example, Adobe Photoshop and Illustrator came out. This software enabled me to develop Leonard's logo in a more refined, illustrative manner, rather than relying on sketches. We threw concepts around, and it started to be interesting to me because his creativity wasn't just the musicianship; there was also a visual and graphic component to it. I could support him in realizing that, both in print and in other specific applications. Because a lot of his self-portraits were very nice but would reproduce comfortably at about the size of a postage stamp. When you go to a larger format, the production becomes an interpretive challenge.

JC: Can you describe what Cohen's interest was in art and design? Was he excited by it, or was it mostly a means to an end in service of the larger effort to make his work as a writer and a performing artist more recognizable? Was there something intrinsically exciting for him in the creative processes of art and design?

MP: He was always interested in visual art, more as a personal expression, and was drawing all the time, as you can see by his notebooks and the contents of his archive. He was always excited to see the final products, particularly in the case of the cloisonné pins, those little tangible objects that are expressions of a concept. The interesting thing about the technology in graphics that emerged

around when we started working together is that a lot of the teamwork of the industry kind of went away. You didn't have to rely so much on outside vendors, typesetters, and people producing photostats and scans of drawings—it all became the responsibility of the person at the desktop. It became similar to his process of creating poetry or song: basically sitting at a table with the notebook and the drawing pads (fig. 1).

JC: So, he used his Mac and Adobe Illustrator as instruments of creativity and to generate ideas?

MP: Yes, he did. Well, Adobe Photoshop, actually—he didn't get into Illustrator that much. He used (the now defunct) MacPaint and MacDraw, as well as scanning software; all the tools are in the paintbox within this one device. If you know what you're doing and you're familiar with the process, you can execute all sorts of things.

JC: Did you instruct Cohen with these tools or was he self-directed?

MP: Mostly he would figure it out on his own. His early Mac came with the revolutionary WYSIWYG [what you see is what you get] format, so that you could see the layout and the composition of the type and the letterforms all there, and then print, scan, and alter it with the feedback of having the printout—seeing it, creating it, revising it, transforming it—and then print another iteration. It was quite exciting because of that more intuitive process. There were not any formidable technical challenges until you got into more specific applications, which I could expedite for him, or in some instances take something that he had roughed out and refine it to the point where it would be successful in other formats. It's analogous to think of the function of a record producer in relation to a musician. I was in charge of shaping the final output. He liked to explore options. We sent things back and forth through emails and refined his ideas that way.

JC: You are describing the versioning that is so common in his writing. It is present in his art-making as well.... You also helped him make these very beautiful and custom-created pigment prints that were produced in limited editions. How did the idea for that come to be?

MP: It was an evolutionary process. After *The Future* tour ended in 1993, I worked with him on *Cohen Live* (fig. 2). He was interested in some old art, from Nicholas Roerich, perhaps—this little church icon in the background—he was playing with it and we were working on posterizing things. This was 1994. And then basically he was incommunicado through the 1990s [while studying Zen Buddhism and becoming ordained at the Mt. Baldy Zen Center in the San Gabriel

FROM TOP LEFT
(clockwise):

Fig. 3 Leonard Cohen,
*Dear Heather*, 2004

Fig. 4 Leonard Cohen,
"Go No More A-Rovin'"
lyrics in *Dear Heather*,
2004

Fig. 5 Leonard Cohen,
Drawings in *Book of
Longing*, 2006

Fig. 6 Philip Glass,
*Book of Longing*, 2007

## GO NO MORE A-ROVING (3:40)

*for Irving Layton*
*Words: Lord Byron (1788-1824)*
*Music: Leonard Cohen*

So we'll go no more a-roving
So late into the night,
Though the heart be still as loving,
And the moon be still as bright.

For the sword outwears its sheath,
And the soul outwears the breast,
And the heart must pause to breathe,
And love itself have rest.

Though the night was made for loving,
And the day returns too soon,
Yet we'll go no more a-roving
By the light of the moon.

*Produced, arranged and performed
by Sharon Robinson
Vocals: L.C. and Sharon Robinson
Tenor Sax: Bob Sheppard
℗ 2004 Old Ideas LLC (BMI).
All Rights Reserved. Used By Permission.
"Irving" after a photo by Lazlo*

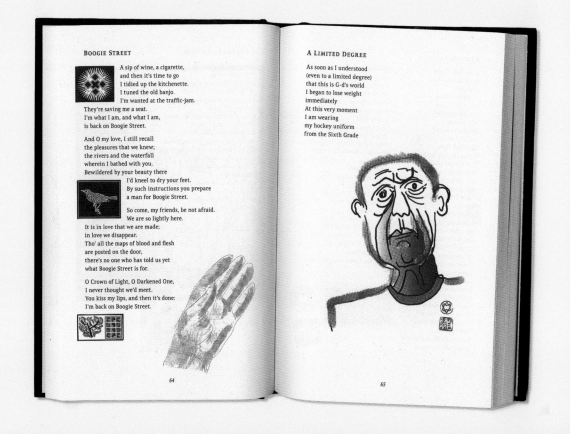

Mountains one hour north of Los Angeles]. In 2000/2001, he worked with Sharon Robinson on *Ten New Songs.* She went up to Baldy a few times, and he came back down to LA a few times. And then in the early 2000s, I worked for him and Anjani Thomas in LA doing various albums. Anjani was getting very interested in Judaism for *The Sacred Names* album and was reading through his notebooks in search of source material for songs that would later make up her 2006 album *Blue Alert.* By 2004, we started to work on *Dear Heather* (fig. 3). This was a much more experimental frame of mind that he was exploring. You see familiar elements emerge, such as his Unified Hearts symbol, and he started to produce Word documents for me with some graphic components. The album's lyrics booklet became a combination of art and text (fig. 4). At one point, I said, "Well, these are interesting—perhaps some other ones we might consider." So, we went into the downstairs storage area in the garage —upstairs was his recording studio—and started to pull file folders out of cabinets, notebooks, prints, drawings, and things he had been doing on his self-portrait experiment from 2002 to 2005. He made these self-portraits, which were digitally created, and I helped him retrieve and refine some of those that were buried away in folders. He wasn't quite conversant with the hierarchical filing system in the computer, but we were able to bring them back to the light of day. There was such a wealth of material that he went into his next creative project with greater graphic content, which became *Book of Longing*, combining many familiar and new images along with the poetry (fig. 5).

JC: So, *Dear Heather* really was a pivotal project?

MP: Yes, it was a formative work in many ways because it was a little freer and more experimental. Tracks like "Morning Glory" are almost improvisational—it's not what you're accustomed to with Leonard's meticulously refined, honed, and polished style. It's a little rougher around the edges where he was trying new things. I felt that he was always freer and more spontaneous in his artwork because it was a personal exercise mostly, and a lot of his drawings are almost like visual jazz to me. He would be free and spontaneous with visual art, as opposed to his more precisely con-trolled and organized musical output. This style worked very well in *Book of Longing.* For that project we would send drawings back and forth through email, and then refine pages, work on cover designs, and the final one was a little different. What really excited him about the project was that I could compose a two-sided dummy with the spine and the binding and, basically, I could give him a book he could take to McClelland & Stewart and places and say, "I have a book of poetry I'm making. Here it is!" I gave him three dummies for his trip to the publishers. That was very exciting to him, the tangible, physical, comprehensive layout was so close to the

final—it was a matter of him having control over the final object, without the intercession of all the intermediate craftspeople.

JC: Was *Book of Longing* the first time he was able to extensively combine the written word and his own imagery?

MP: Well, there was *Dear Heather* and on a smaller scale his self-portraits, which would have the aphorisms or thoughts of the day. I think he felt that this more spontaneous exercise was liberating, and these works started to generate significant interest. That led us toward Luminato and his collaboration with Philip Glass and the song cycle of *Book of Longing* (fig. 6), which was staged with projec-tions and with scrims featuring printed art; the visuals in conjunction with the music and the performances of the spoken—sung—words was a nice multimedia effect for him.

At this point, I think that Leonard began to consider that perhaps his visual art wasn't just purely a personal endeavour, that maybe this could be explored in a more formal way, thanks to a gallerist from Manchester, Richard Goodall, who had been prompting Leonard to present his art as fine art. It was a matter of working with, refining, and selecting the imagery, and then finding a process and a vendor that could execute these in the formats that made sense. Once we'd narrowed in on a few dozen pieces to get them in shape so that they would reproduce correctly, I helped to expedite the final production process for him. For the final exhibition prints, Nash Editions always did the work and really made a significant difference. They had ultra-large formats, and they could print to a very high standard, with gorgeous colour saturation.

Leonard was gratified that the Luminato show turned out really well and the prints were generally really well received. We went up to Toronto and he was pleased with the exhibition. The Drabinsky Gallery did a nice catalogue, they had a very good turnout, and a lot of people were interested. We would go around at the time and start to see his artwork showing up as graffiti on underpasses and bridges. It was a trip to go down by the Distillery District and see the artworks on the walls.

JC: With the printmaking, were you always using inkjet?

MP: Yes, it was the only option for the larger format. I set up a proofing station at the office of Robert Kory [Cohen's manager] with an iMac, large-scale scanner, and an Epson photo printer for large format, and I would print them to size. Leonard was pretty excited by the output because this went far beyond the little desktop screen and the proofer he had. It was useful, too, because with some of the scans we wanted to get so large that we would have to print it on two sheets and splice it together. In a few cases, Leonard thought it would be interesting to bleed the image to the

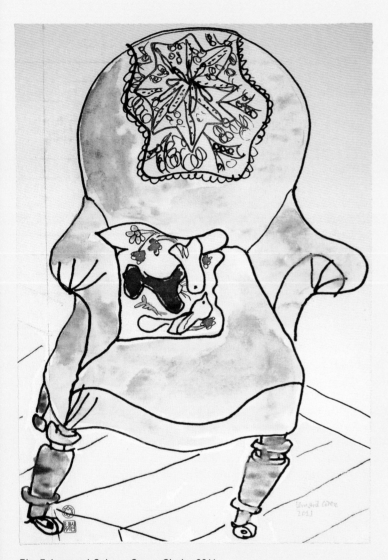

Fig. 7 Leonard Cohen, *Green Chair*, 2011

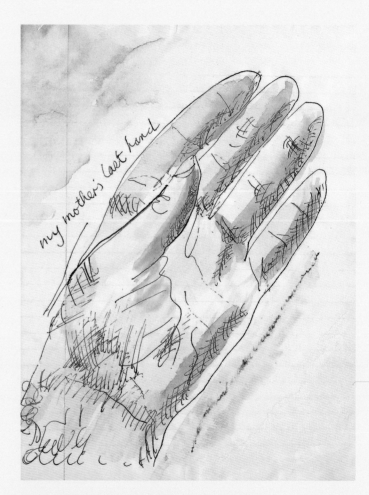

Fig. 8 Leonard Cohen, *My Mother's Last Hand (Watercolour Notebook)*, 1980–1985

edge of the page. So we went forward with those particular images in that style.

Once we had made a proof and said, this looks like a valid concept, we would send a new file to the printer. Leonard made some minor revisions to a couple when he saw the first proof. But for the most part, what we wanted was what we got, and then it was just off to the races. We would have the flexibility to basically print them in batches on demand, rather than doing a full print run as a standard lithograph, all at once. I would have to work in a curatorial manner to keep track of the orders from the galleries, in Oslo, Richard Goodall's in Manchester, and the various places. Vancouver had a good run for a while. I think we ended up selling something north of 1,200 prints to collectors.

JC: How would you characterize Cohen's relationship to this whole phenomenon of the visual arts, as more of his artwork surfaced and was visible to his audience?

MP: At first maybe he was a little bemused to be taken seriously, but he was gratified by the interest and began to be more comfortable with that dimension of his work. He would go away sometimes and come back with some new drawings and say, you know, this might be something that could work. I never extracted things from him unwillingly. A couple of times during a tour he would come back on hiatus and make some drawings that we then transformed into prints. It was frustrating to him, occasionally, not to have enough time to devote to drawing and painting, since the rigours of the road demanded so much time and energy. He was like Napoleon to his generals: "Ask me for anything but time."

JC: Are any of Cohen's drawings particularly satisfying to you, and if so, for what reason?

MP: I thought that he was in a very creative phase when he was doing the watercolours in the notebooks that became *End of the Day*, *Woman and Horse*, *Green Chair* (fig. 7), and *My Mother's Last Hand* (fig. 8). That was a very fertile time for him. I always found the self-portraits particularly interesting because they were freer and more spontaneous. Some of his later drawings were really quite good, too; when I saw them, I didn't hesitate to try to bring them into an edition format. It was fun to see the spontaneity of it all.

JC: Were there any artists who particularly influenced him?

MP: He always said that he felt like his own "art" drew more praise than he deserved. He said his friend Morton Rosengarten was the real artist in his group and that Morton never received the recognition that Leonard felt he warranted.

JC: Was there a particular high point for you in your collaboration with Cohen over the years?

MP: Obviously, the first one, with all the work on *The Future*, felt like moving into a new area for me. The explorations and discovery in the process of *Dear Heather*, which pretty well seamlessly evolved into the more elaborate and much larger scale *Book of Longing*, uncovering such a vast amount of visual art and in conjunction with the poetry, and developing that into a format that was satisfying on a visual and the written level—that was certainly a high point. As the [2008–2013 world] tour went on, that became very interesting indeed because it was another chance to incorporate a lot of familiar things. To do a sixty-foot-tall scrim and also have one with the image of *End of the Day* and *Woman and Horse* (fig. 9)—to see it deployed effectively as integral to this staging was very gratifying.

Leonard was very determined to give all he had musically, but he also wanted to provide something meaningful to the audience that they could take away. So merchandising was a chance to apply tangibly a lot of his familiar things; for example, embroidered patches, the access passes, lanyards, cloisonné pins, keychains, and other products (see pages 115–117). Also, the tour book incorporated art and reflected some of the integration of his art and his lyrics. That was extremely gratifying, too, and on a larger scope than so much else before.

JC: And today, do you continue to work on promotional products, box sets, and so on?

MP: I recently worked with Sony on a compilation disc that's coming out, but that is more the concert photography than artwork. And one of the sadly gratifying things was the opportunity to design Leonard's tombstone in Montreal. I was really honoured to do that, but very sad too, of course. I worked with Adam Cohen on that.

JC: Cohen described his own artwork as "acceptable decorations." What do you think he meant by that phrase?

MP: Well, it's the concluding couplet to his poem "If There Were No Paintings," which pretty well summed up the humble approach to his artwork. Reading through the poem, which he insisted should be printed and displayed with every exhibition that we did, in Norway and Finland, and Manchester... I think it is an apt description of how he felt and approached his art. He stayed humble and didn't take himself so seriously.

JC: I know that Cohen enjoyed the act of drawing throughout his life. Do you think his style changed much over the years?

Fig. 9 Scrim projection of Leonard Cohen's *Woman and Horse* (1980–1985) during his world tour concert in Berlin, 2013

Leonard Cohen and Michael Petit, *Leonard Cohen: The Future World Tour* t-shirt, 1993

MP: I don't know if I'd pin him down to any particular style. I think in the 1980s and 1990s he was working from some photographic sources where he would manipulate drawings, the old lighter fluid transfer kind of thing, and then sketch from that. But the self-portraits are him and his trusty Wacom tablet, his mirror, and his Mac, and that's pretty loose, I would say. You can look at the self-portraits and see they're very loose for the most part.

JC: Is there anything you would add in closing?

MP: Leonard was a remarkable, multifaceted talent. I was there watching him assemble things, and he had expertise with the software for arranging the songs and the composition that he would so diligently work on. I witnessed his consideration for his audience regarding performance. When we were working on *Popular Problems* and *Old Ideas,* he was in the later leg of a tour and was going to do a concert in Quebec. Every time I'd go over to show him a layout, he'd be listening to "La Manic" because he wanted to get the intonation right; he wanted to nail it for the Québécois audience, to make sure that he got the song right. His consideration for the audience was very profound.

JC: And he seemed to take abundant care in all of his creative activities?

MP: Yes, in everything he did. When I was working with the layout for *Dear Heather* in 2004, it was a rather tumultuous time for Leonard. I went to show him a layout one afternoon and the screen door was open and I heard him playing the guitar. It was really nice. I didn't want to knock. I just wanted to listen. When he stopped, and I knocked, he was holding his guitar, and with a broad smile he said: "I've been struggling to get this introduction for 'Nightingale' right"—one of the tracks on *Dear Heather*—"and I think I've really nailed it." For weeks, at the same time, we were doing the lyrics, and there was an image of a nightingale for that lyric. We went through twelve different versions: it was blue and red and green, and bigger and smaller, and he would send me emails, saying, "Here's another layout for that relentless nightingale." He would sweat the small stuff. It all mattered to him. With his artwork, a digital workflow enabled him to exercise a level of control and meticulous craftsmanship similar to what he was accustomed to doing with his writing and musical efforts.

—

MICHAEL PETIT is an independent graphic designer based in Pasadena, California, who worked with Leonard Cohen on numerous projects from 1992 to 2016.

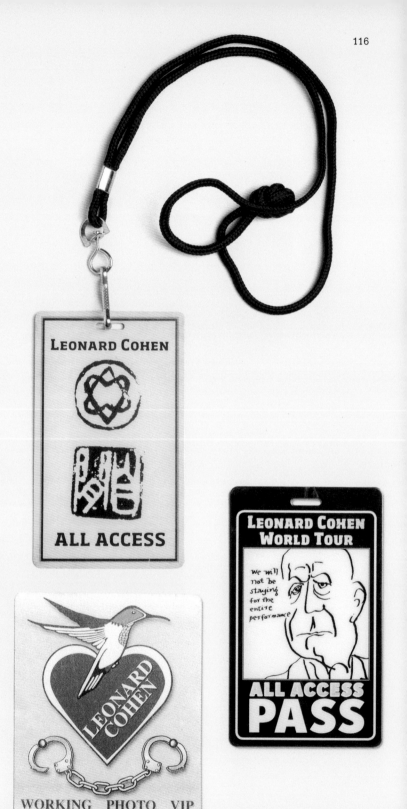

Leonard Cohen and Michael Petit, Concert merchandise, 1992–2008

# A BLAZE OF LIGHT IN EVERY WORD

## REVISION AND THE QUEST FOR PERFECTION IN LEONARD COHEN'S WRITING PROCESS

Alan Light

"Sometimes I think that I would go along with the old Beat philosophy, 'First thought, best thought.' But it never worked for me. There hardly is a first thought. It's all sweat."
—Leonard Cohen

The cliché perception of writing pop songs rests on the flash of inspiration—spontaneous, unfiltered, pure. In 2021, viewers around the world were transfixed by the previously unseen 1969 studio footage of the Beatles in Peter Jackson's documentary *Get Back*, and one of the scenes that got the most attention was a clip of Paul McCartney idly sitting by himself and strumming his bass, seemingly improvising a basic melody and tossing out words that suddenly coalesced into the song that gave the film its title, and just weeks after its recording, entered the charts at number one.

It is a staggering moment to witness, setting a preposterous bar for aspiring songwriters, and an extreme case of what we've come to expect because of the depiction so often seen in movies and on television. The creation of "Get Back" is also the polar opposite of the process exemplified by one of the other pillars of songwriting in the rock 'n' roll era, Leonard Cohen.

Unlike the Beatles, who learned their craft primarily from studying and performing other songs, Cohen was a published poet and novelist before pursuing a music career, and perhaps as a result of this tradition, he laboured long and hard over each line, each word, in every song that he wrote. If "Get Back" is an example of writing as sudden revelation—plucked from thin air, conjured from mystic vision—Cohen's work is instead the triumph of precision, elegance, and revision.

As far back as 1966, Cohen spoke of the focus and patience his writing demanded. "It takes a fantastic inner compulsion [to write]," he said to Jon Ruddy for the Canadian magazine *Maclean's*. "Nobody writes who doesn't really drive himself. I feel secretly that I am much more highly disciplined than anybody I meet."[1]

Over the decades, Cohen's struggle with his own creativity became a central part of his story, as he recounted toiling over individual songs for many years, filling page after page with rough verses, striving for an elusive literary perfection. In 1992, Wayne Robins of *Newsday* referred to him as "the laureate of creative agony."[2] And if you read enough Cohen interviews back to back, his torment almost starts to feel like schtick or, as we might put it today, a humblebrag. Especially in his later years, he stopped short of asking for our sympathy, but the sense prevails of how hard-fought his efforts were, and the cost of serving such a demanding muse. He even noted that others might find consolation in his labour: "Some people may find it encouraging to see how slow and dismal and painstaking is the process," he once said.[3]

But with the Art Gallery of Ontario's exhibit *Leonard Cohen: Everybody Knows*—the first museum exhibition to present the holdings of the Leonard Cohen Family Trust—we are finally able to see these efforts up close, to examine some of the legendary notebooks and observe immortal lyrics taking shape. Cohen's process of constant revision comes alive before our eyes, with instantly recognizable lines and phrases leaping off a page of unfamiliar words, and letters or journal entries revealing how this work was endlessly churning through Cohen's mind.

Cohen often referred to the act of writing as "blackening the pages." ("I blacken pages. I'm not a writer," he told the *Guardian* in 1970. "The writing is the ash of the experience.")[4] As the items in *Leonard Cohen: Everybody Knows* illustrate, that blackening was not just a matter of scrawling down words but also of adding, crossing out, moving sections around. It gives a tangible, physical sense of the work— although Cohen happily embraced writing on a computer when it became an option, these handwritten sheets show the traces of a poet's mind in action.

"I find that easy versions of the song arrive first," he told Paul Zollo of *SongTalk* magazine in 1993. "Although they might be able to stand as songs, they can't stand as songs that I can sing. So to find a song that I can sing, to engage my interest, to penetrate my boredom with myself and my disinterest in my own opinions, to penetrate those barriers, the song has to speak to me with a certain urgency. To be able to find that song that I can be interested in takes many versions and it takes a lot of uncovering."[5]

Nor was this impulse something that he could easily turn off. "It takes me a great deal of time to find out what the song is," he told Zollo. "So, I am working most of the time."[6] A handwritten journal entry (fig. 1) included in the exhibit dated "Imperial Hotel, Asmara Ethiopia, March 21, 1974" gives some sense of a songwriter's daily existence:

> Washed my white shirt. Hung it to dry in the sun on my balcony. Sang for an hour. Getting close to Desmos' Song. First two verses of Chelsea Hotel will do; delete the third. Possible lines for third chorus of War Song. Shirt is almost dry. (4 pm)

"The process of songwriting for me is arduous and painful because I have to go to the place where the song is," Cohen told Thom Jurek of Detroit's *Metro Times* in 1993. "I have to inhabit it and allow it to have its way with me. I have to write perfectly many verses that get thrown away because they are imperfect for a particular song, and it takes time and patience and tears to get there."[7]

He expanded on this idea when speaking to the *Philadelphia Inquirer*'s Tom Moon that same year. "I've only learned one thing from writing songs, and that is, if you stay with it long enough, the song will yield," Cohen said. "You burn away those versions of yourself, your courage, and your modesty until you get something irreducible."[8]

More succinctly, Cohen put it this way in a 1988 KCRW radio interview with Kristine McKenna: "I had to revise my work until it became the only possible song I could sing."[9]

There's a story that Cohen told, on various occasions over the years, to illustrate the contrast between his own writing process and that of his friend and inspiration Bob Dylan. He said that he and Dylan once met for coffee when they both found themselves in Paris in the mid-1980s. Dylan expressed admiration for Cohen's then-obscure composition "Hallelujah" and asked how long it took to write. Cohen replied that it took him a couple of years ("I lied, actually. It was more than a couple of years").[10]

Cohen responded by praising a song of Dylan's on the 1984 album *Infidels* called "I and I," and inquired how long he needed to write that one. Dylan responded, "Fifteen minutes."

However apocryphal this anecdote is, or how literally we are to take either of their answers, the stark difference between Dylan's desire for creative immediacy and Cohen's painstaking craft is accurate, and significant. In his conversation with Paul Zollo, Cohen offered some fascinating thoughts about Dylan's language.

"At a certain point, when the Jews were first commanded to raise an altar, the commandment was on unhewn stone," he said. "Apparently the god that wanted that particular altar didn't want slick, didn't want smooth. He wanted an unhewn stone placed on another unhewn stone. Maybe then you go looking for stones that fit. Maybe that was the process that God wanted the makers of this altar to undergo.

"Now I think Dylan has lines, hundreds of great lines that have the feel of unhewn stone. But they really fit in there. But they're not smoothed out. It's inspired but not polished."[11]

And although the Paris story was something that Cohen clearly played for laughs, there is undoubtedly a good deal of truth in his response regarding "Hallelujah" and its own lengthy smoothing out. The song, first released on 1984's *Various Positions* album, is both his most famous creation—a staple of movie soundtracks, religious ceremonies, and televised singing competitions—and his most celebrated example of extended editing and refining. Cohen has repeatedly described the agony that this one lyric gave him. "I filled two notebooks," he once said, "and I remember being in the Royalton Hotel [in New York], on the carpet in my underwear, banging my head on the floor and saying, 'I can't finish this song.'"[12]

When his album *Old Ideas* came out in 2012, rather than do interviews, Cohen appeared at a few listening events in major cities, allowing journalists to hear the album in full and then taking questions. In London, the playback was held in the basement of a Mayfair Hotel, and Jarvis Cocker, debonair front man of the band Pulp, served as the moderator. These many years later, Cohen was still talking about the misery that "Hallelujah" caused him.

"I wrote 'Hallelujah' over the space of at least four years," he said. (Elsewhere, he has also said that it was at least five years.) "I wrote many, many verses. I don't know if it was eighty, maybe more or a little less."[13]

Imperial Hotel
Asmara, Ethiopia
March 21, 1974

Excellent lunch at Albergo Italiano. Washed my
white shirt. Hung it to dry in the sun on my balcony.
Sang for an hour. Getting close to Desmos' Song.
First two verses of Chelsea Hotel will do; delete the third.
Passable lines for third chorus of War Song. Shirt
is almost dry. (4 p.m.)

Rented bicycle (~~~~~$5 u.s). Bought grey material.
Suit will be ready Saturday.

Soaked grey words, hung them out in the evening
air.

Fig. 1 Leonard Cohen, *Imperial Hotel Journal Entry*, 1974

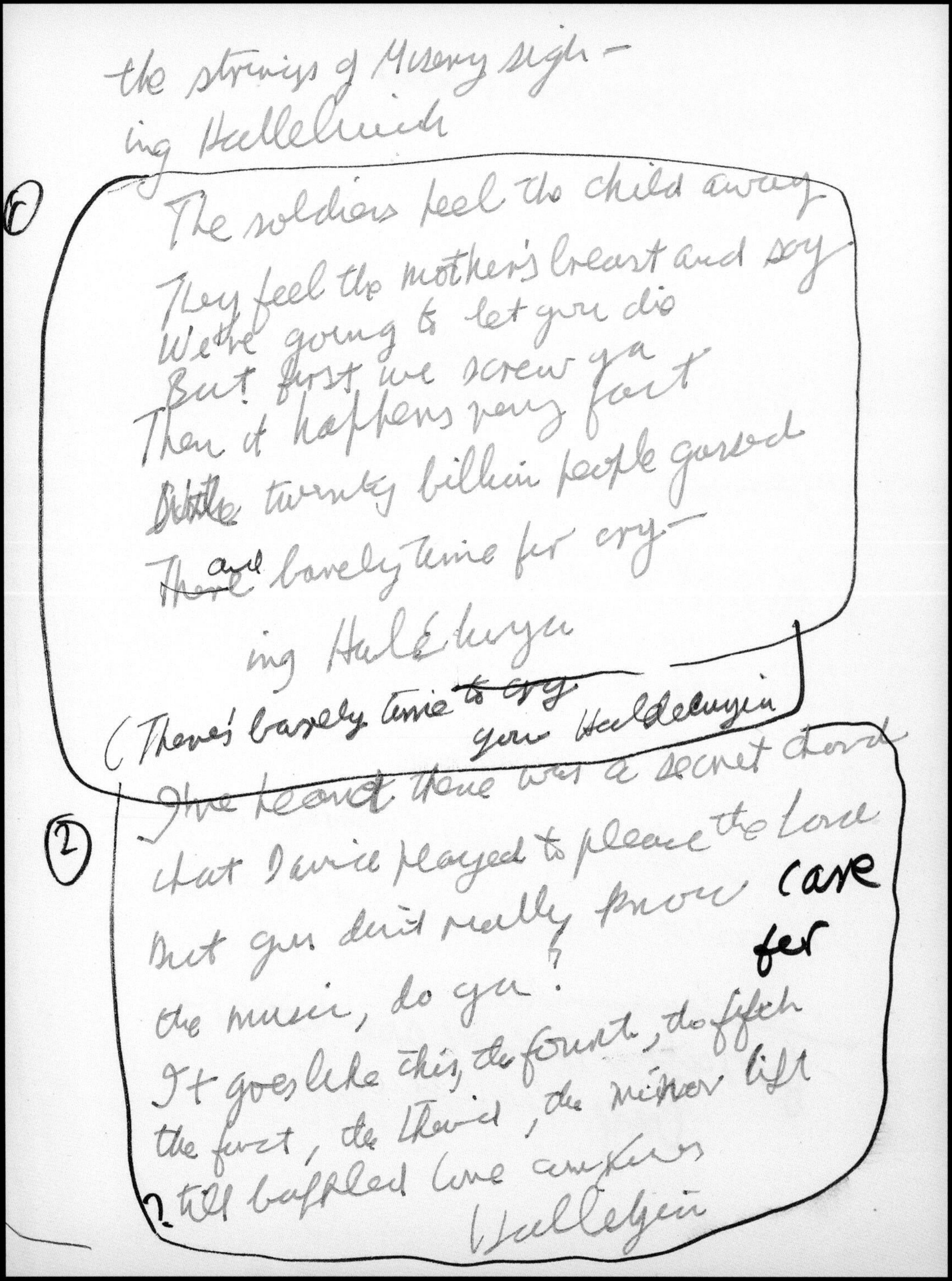

the strings of Misery sigh—
ing Hallelujah

① The soldiers feel the child away
They feel the mother's breast and say
We're going to let you die
But first we screw ya
Then it happens very fast
Little twenty billion people gassed
There *and* barely time for cry—

ing Hallelujah

( There's barely time ~~to cry~~
                    your Hallelujah

~~I've heard there was a secret chord~~
② that I *once* played to please the Lord
But you don't really ~~know~~ *care* *for*
the music, do ya?
It goes like this, the fourth, the fifth
the first, the third, the minor lift
? the baffled king composing
                    Hallelujah

Fig. 2  Leonard Cohen, *"Hallelujah" Notebook*, 1983–1984

*Leonard Cohen: Everybody Knows* includes a selection from the mythical "Hallelujah" notebooks, and even this glimpse is riveting. In this undated page (fig. 2), the beloved opening lines are intact, though a note offers the options of "You don't really know the music" and the eventual "You don't care for music," while a scribble on the left-hand page also presents the possibility of "You don't really know the answer, do ya."

The line in the first verse that would become "the minor fall, the major lift" isn't worked out yet; here it is "the first, the third, the minor lift." Also, the "baffled king composing hallelujah" hasn't yet made his appearance—in that spot within the text, Cohen wrote "the baffled love awakens hallelujah," and on the facing page, he's getting closer, with "the baffled heart composing hallelujah."

In addition to these precision edits, we are also presented with one of the unused verses, and it's an image far darker than the message of perseverance through heartbreak that defines the final song:

> The soldiers peel the child away
> They feel the mother's breast and say
> We're going to let you die
> But first we screw ya
> Then it happens very fast
> Twenty billion people gassed
> There's barely time for crying hallelujah

Although scenes of war and apocalypse appear throughout Cohen's work, these are not themes we associate with the personal battlefield depicted in "Hallelujah." Here, Cohen's notes for the song are certainly a long way from the "hallelujah of the orgasm" that Jeff Buckley found in his interpretation, a version that helped propel it to the status of modern standard. But Cohen put in those years of work on the song attempting to hone its precise mood and message, piling up all of his thoughts and then shaving down to the essence of the lyrics; to return to the metaphor he used regarding Bob Dylan's style, Cohen approaches his writing like a sculptor cutting away all the unnecessary parts of a stone to find the shape he wants.

"My tiny trouble," Cohen said to Jarvis Cocker, "is that before I can discard a verse, I have to write it. I have to work on it, and I have to polish it and bring it to as close to finished as I can. It's only then that I can discard it."[14]

He used similar language in his 1993 interview with Thom Jurek. "I have to discard versions of myself, and versions of the songs, until I can get to a situation where I can defend every word, every line," he said. "But that place often involves a real shattering of equanimity, or of balance.... I have to go to this naked and raw place. And it usually involves the breakdown of my personality, and I flip out."[15]

Producer John Lissauer says that when Cohen recorded "Hallelujah" for the *Various Positions* album, he came to the studio with a completed edit—he knew which verses he wanted to record and didn't deviate from that selection.[16] But the process of revision didn't end when the song was cut or the album was released; particularly on this song that had haunted its writer for so long, Cohen continued to rework the lyrics on stage, finding his way toward a version that resonated the strongest in performance.

When John Cale asked Cohen's office for a set of the lyrics to "Hallelujah" so that he could record it for a Cohen tribute album, they faxed him pages of verses, both used and unused. He edited them, and that is the version that Buckley heard and on which he based his cover. Later, Cohen would incorporate the words that those singers had chosen into his own performances of the song, still striving to solve the mystery of "Hallelujah" many decades later.

"That's the question I ask myself about all my material at a certain point," he told Alberto Manzano of Spain's *El Europeo* magazine in 1993. "Is it really true? It doesn't matter whether it's a successful metaphor; what matters is whether it honestly reflects my predicament."[17]

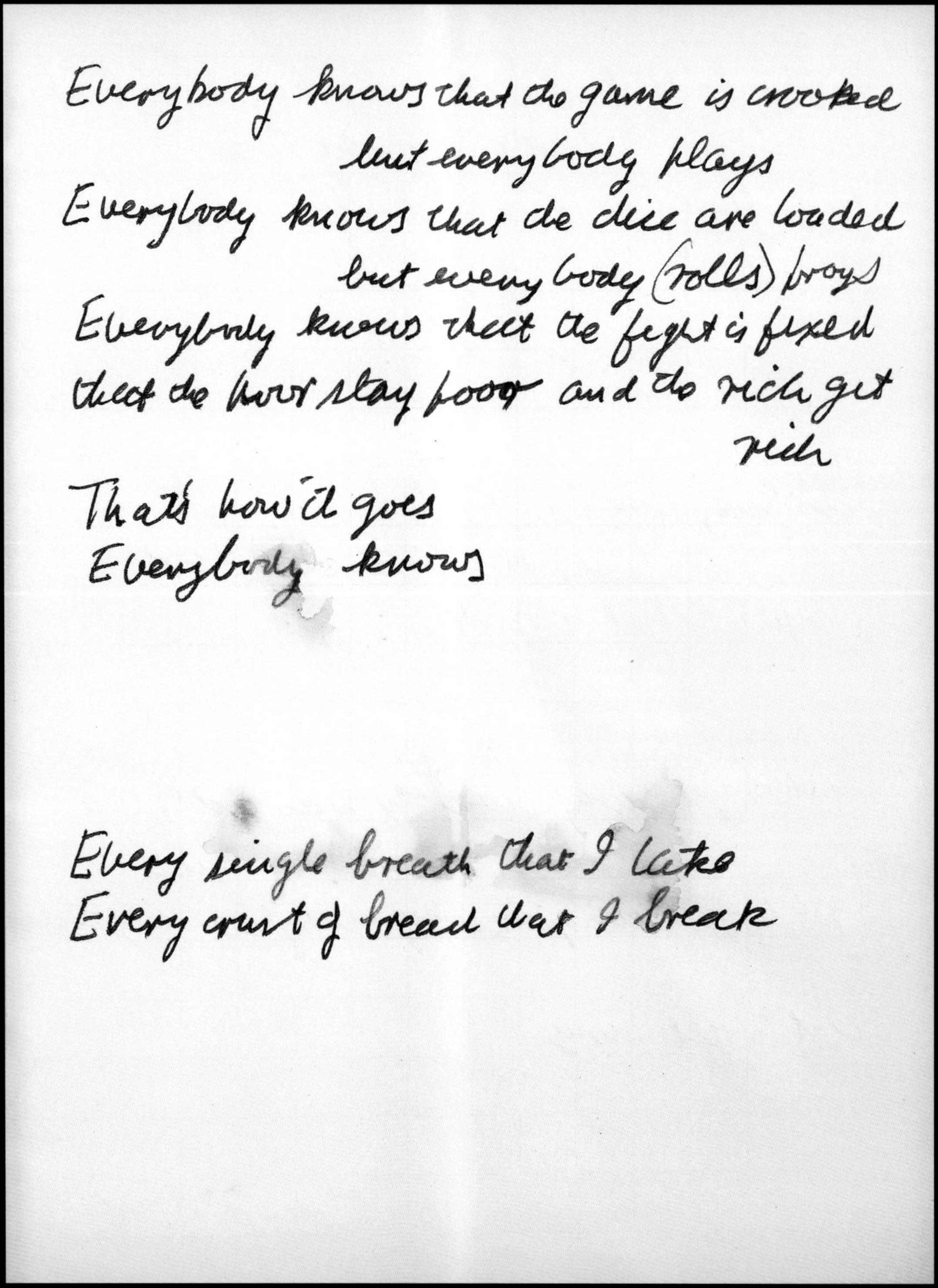

Everybody knows that the game is crooked
              but everybody plays
Everybody knows that the dice are loaded
              but everybody (rolls) prays
Everybody knows that the fight is fixed
that the poor stay poor and the rich get
                              rich

That's how it goes
Everybody knows

Every single breath that I take
Every crust of bread that I break

Fig. 3  Leonard Cohen, "Everybody Knows," 1987

Two other song manuscripts are included in the *Leonard Cohen: Everybody Knows* exhibit, taken from the albums that unexpectedly put him back on the map in the late 1980s and early 1990s. The song that gives the exhibition its title was a highlight of 1988's *I'm Your Man*, Cohen's return to recording after the disappointing reaction to *Various Positions*. It's a bleakly comedic account of the social condition, a commentary on politics and class that grows more relevant with each passing year.

In this case, the draft (fig. 3) is close to the final edit:

> Everybody knows that the game is crooked,
>     but everybody plays
> Everybody knows that the dice are loaded, but
>     everybody (rolls) prays
> Everybody knows that the fight is fixed
> That the poor stay poor and the rich get rich
> That's how it goes
> Everybody knows

The first line was scrapped (though its theme remains true to the song), and the second line was reworked into the opening of the ultimate recording—"Everybody knows that the dice are loaded / Everybody rolls with their fingers crossed."

And then, at the bottom of the page, this couplet—

> Every single breath that I take
> Every crust of bread that I break

—which doesn't seem to appear anywhere in Cohen's catalogue; we are left to speculate whether it was intended for "Everybody Knows" or was a stray note for something else in the works.

Cohen had been grappling with this song for many years. He told Manzano, "I've been writing that song since the early eighties, maybe late seventies." It apparently started life as a different song, titled "Waiting for the Miracle" (a version of which was released a few years later on his next album, 1992's *The Future*). "[It] wasn't a bad song," he said. "Nonetheless, I found I couldn't sing it because I questioned whether I really was waiting for the miracle."[18]

In 2006, he described the song's origins and transformation to Shelagh Rogers of the CBC. "That guy [in the song] was a kind of know-it-all who'd been there and done that and seen it all," he said. "I think that was how it began but then under the tyranny of rhyme, other lines emerged that I could never possibly come up with." He expressed appreciation, and a certain wonder, at some of the lines and images that emerged during the rewriting. "It's not that I don't sweat over it because I do. I sweat over every word. And it takes me a long time to bring these songs to completion. But when these little gifts appear, you're still wonderfully surprised and grateful."[19]

Keep in mind, Cohen's process wasn't simply a matter of refining the words; as his edit progressed, the rhythm and structure of the song were being altered as well. "When the lyric begins to be revised, of course, the line can't carry it with its new nuance or its new meaning," he told Zollo. "And generally, the musical line has to change, which involves changing the next musical line, which involves changing the next lyrical line, so the process is mutual and painstaking and slow."[20]

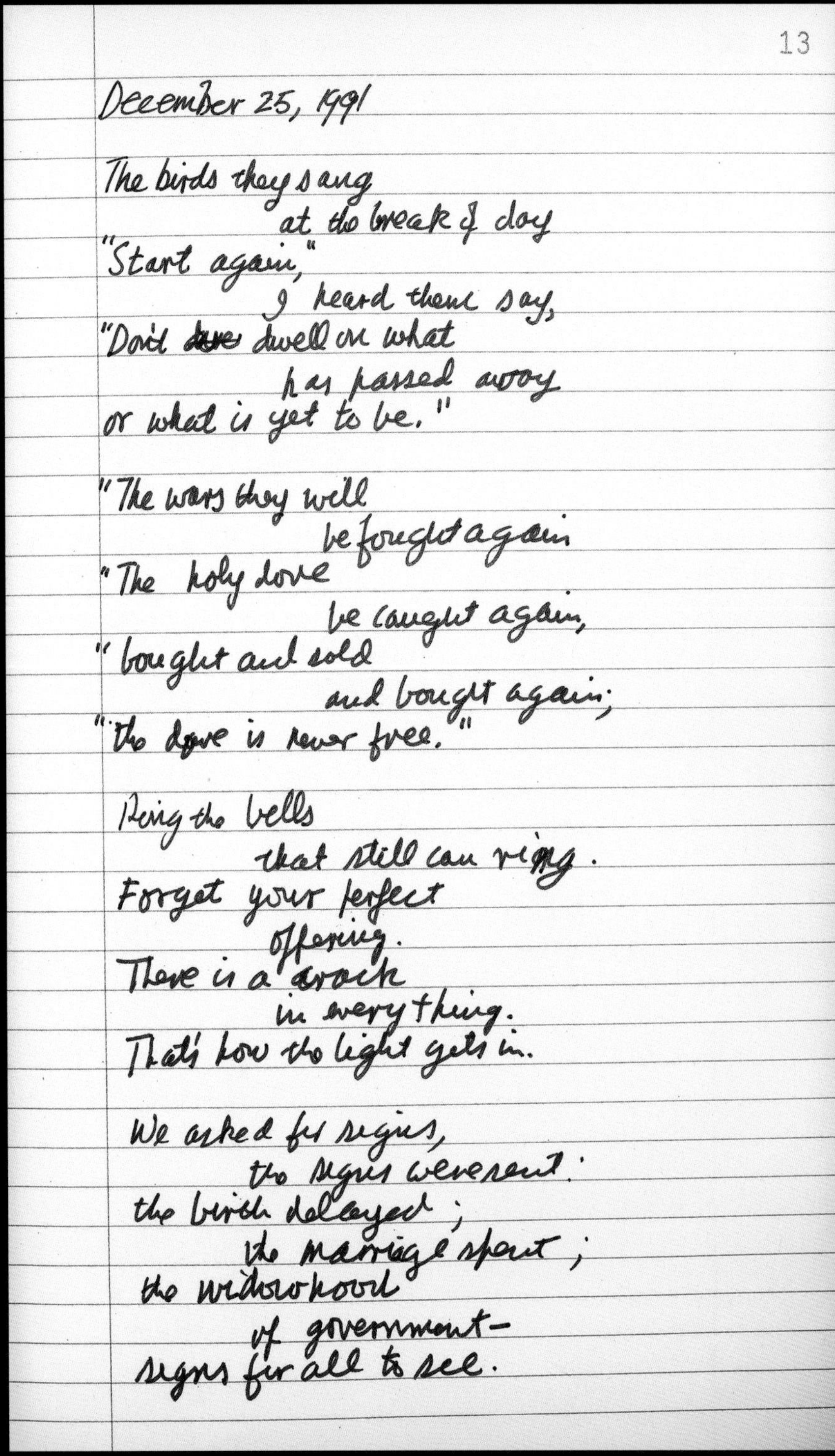

December 25, 1991

The birds they sang
            at the break of day
"Start again,"
            I heard them say,
"Don't ~~dare~~ dwell on what
            has passed away
or what is yet to be."

"The wars they will
            be fought again
"The holy dove
            be caught again,
"bought and sold
            and bought again;
"the dove is never free."

Ring the bells
            that still can ring.
Forget your perfect
            offering.
There is a crack
            in every thing.
That's how the light gets in.

We asked for signs,
            the signs were sent:
the birth delayed;
            the marriage spent;
the widowhood
            of government—
signs for all to see.

Fig. 4  Leonard Cohen, "Anthem," 1991

Finally, we see a page from the notebook that contains the lyrics to "Anthem" (fig. 4), the centrepiece of *The Future* and a song widely considered to be one of Cohen's masterpieces. Based on Kabbalistic images, and offering a (literal) moment of Zen within an album inspired by the chaos of the era (from the fall of the Berlin Wall to the Los Angeles riots, visible from Cohen's home), the song includes the frequently quoted line "There is a crack in everything/ That's how the light gets in"—about which Cohen once said, "That sums it up; it is as close to a credo as I've come."[21]

December 25, 1991

The birds they sang at the break of day
"Start again," I heard them say,
"Don't dwell on what has passed away
Or what is yet to be."

"The wars they will be fought again
"The holy dove be caught again,
"Bought and sold and bought again;
"The dove is never free."

Ring the bells that can still ring.
Forget your perfect offering.
There is a crack in everything.
That's how the light gets in.

We asked for signs, the signs were sent.
The birth delayed; the marriage spent;
The widowhood of government—
Signs for all to see.

Perhaps the most crucial information on this page is the date; this clearly represents a (near) finished version of the lyrics, and Cohen would begin recording the album the following month. There's only one significant change between these written lines and the final recording, "the birth delayed" will become "the birth betrayed."

But the cleanliness of this sheet—nothing crossed out, no extra notes or alternate phrases—comes at the end of a long struggle with the words to "Anthem." When Alberto Manzano pointed out that some of the lyrics had been used in the song "The Bells," which Cohen had written for Canadian musician Lewis Furey's 1985 film *Night Magic*, Cohen explained: "I'd always been trying to record this song," he said. "I've been trying to record this song for *Various Positions*—several versions that didn't work. I prepared a version for *I'm Your Man*...that I couldn't use in the end because some words were wrong, the feeling was wrong, the time was wrong. Finally in this record I tried it several times."[22]

He reiterated to Paul Zollo that "Anthem" took a decade to write and was recorded multiple times for his previous albums, and that he had been "recycling" lines from his efforts into many other songs. "There was something wrong with the lyric, there was something wrong with the tune, there was something wrong with the tempo. There was a lie somewhere in there. There was a disclosure that I was refusing to make."[23]

"Anthem" is one example of a lyric that eventually "yielded" for Cohen after extended exertion. As the latter stages of his career went on, he sometimes indicated that his efforts had relaxed a bit, or at least that he had made peace with his own process. In 2001, he said to j. poet of *Pulse* magazine that "it's gotten easier since I've accepted the fact that I sweat over every word."[24]

But the endless revision and perpetual editing, drafting, and altering lyrics that defined Cohen's work remained with him until the end. In 2011, he told *Mojo* magazine's Sylvie Simmons (who was also in the process of writing her authorized Cohen biography, *I'm Your Man*) of one unfinished song that he had been working on for years. "I've got the melody, and it's a guitar tune, a really good tune, and I have tried year after year to find the right words," he said. "The song bothers me so much that I've actually started a journal chronicling my failures to address this obsessive concern with this melody. I would really like to have it on the next record, but I felt that for the past two or three records, maybe four."[25]

Cohen played another melody for Simmons on the synthesizer, saying it was kicking around for "five or ten years." He told her that "The Treaty," one of the songs on the *Old Ideas* album, had been in play "easily for fifteen years," while he had been working on another, "Born in Chains," since 1988.

"It's not the siege of Stalingrad," he said, "but these are hard nuts to crack."[26]

Over time, Cohen became aware that his frequent references to the difficulties of writing might start to sound overblown. "We're talking in a world where guys go down into the mines, chewing coca and spending all day in backbreaking labour," he said to the *Guardian*'s Dorian Lynskey in 2012. "We're in a world where there's famine and hunger and people are dodging bullets and having their nails pulled out in dungeons so it's very hard for me to place any high value on the work that I do to write a song. Yeah, I work hard but compared to what?"[27]

Yet, as modest and self-deprecating as he was, he took pride in his work, and in the labour required to get as close as he could to the images and language he sought. His explanations of the wrestling required to deliver his songs were not an attempt to further romanticize the creative process but to place them in the context of the work that we all must do—like another poet-turned-musician, Patti Smith, who recently told me, "I don't think of myself as a giant rock star or an icon or anything like that; I think of myself as someone who has the privilege to do this job, and the responsibility, and I do it the best I can, no matter what the circumstances."[28]

Unlike the working-class Smith, Cohen was raised in privilege, but they shared a sense that no matter how glamorous their lives appeared, writing and performing is a job that needs to be done like any other. "Why shouldn't my work be hard?" he said to Paul Zollo. "Almost everybody's work is hard. One is distracted by this notion that there is such a thing as inspiration, that it comes fast and easy. And some people are graced by that style. I'm not. So I have to work as hard as any stiff, to come up with the payload.... To find something that really touches and addresses my attention, I have to do a lot of hard, manual work."[29]

"I was born like this / I had no choice," Leonard Cohen sang in his classic "Tower of Song." For Cohen, as for any great artist, this was accurate, and critical—there was really nothing else he could have done once he was called to making art, no plan B. And for him, that mission extended to every song, every line, every word he wrote. This was the only truth that he knew.

"Mostly my idea of a song is, when you feel like singing and this is your song," he said to the pioneering rock journalist Paul Williams in a 1975 *Crawdaddy!* interview. "It's not what songs *should* be, not choosing; this is the song you make because it's the only one you *can* make, this is the one that is yours. The fact is that you feel like singing, and this is the song that you know."[30]

---

ALAN LIGHT is a music journalist, author, and radio host. He is the former Editor-in-Chief of *Vibe* and *Spin* magazines and a former Senior Writer at *Rolling Stone*. He contributes frequently to the *New York Times* and the *Wall Street Journal*. His book *The Holy or the Broken: Leonard Cohen, Jeff Buckley, and the Unlikely Ascent of "Hallelujah"* was the inspiration for the 2022 documentary *Hallelujah: Leonard Cohen, A Journey, A Song.*

1. In Jon Ruddy, "Is the World (or Anybody) Ready for Leonard Cohen?" *Maclean's,* October 1, 1966, archive.macleans.ca/article/1966/10/1/is-the-world-or-anybody-ready-for-leonard-cohen-.

2. Wayne Robins, "The Loneliness of the Long-Suffering Folkie," *Newsday,* November 22, 1992.

3. In Paul Zollo, "Leonard Cohen: Inside the Tower of Song," *SongTalk,* April 1993.

4. In Hugh Hebert, "From the Archive, 29 August 1970: An Interview with Leonard Cohen," *Guardian,* August 29, 2013, theguardian.com/theguardian/2013/aug/29/leonard-cohen-interview-1970.

5. In Zollo, "Leonard Cohen."

6. In Zollo, "Leonard Cohen."

7. In Thom Jurek, "The Prophet of Love Looks into the Abyss: A Conversation with Leonard Cohen," *Metro Times,* August 18, 1993.

8. In Tom Moon, "Painstaking Effort Pays Off in Leonard Cohen's Future," *Philadelphia Inquirer,* January 4, 1993.

9. In Kristine McKenna, *Eight Hours to Harry,* KCRW-FM, October 1988.

10. In Zollo, "Leonard Cohen."

11. In Zollo, "Leonard Cohen."

12. In Neil McCormick, "Leonard Cohen: Hallelujah!" *Telegraph,* June 14, 2008, telegraph.co.uk/culture/music/3554289/Leonard-Cohen-Hallelujah.html.

13. In Alan Light, *The Holy or the Broken: Leonard Cohen, Jeff Buckley, and the Unlikely Ascent of "Hallelujah"* (New York: Atria Books, 2012), 3.

14. In Light, *The Holy or the Broken.*

15. In Jurek, "The Prophet of Love."

16. Light, *The Holy or the Broken,* 17.

17. In Alberto Manzano, "The Future," *El Europeo,* Spring 1993.

18. In Alberto Manzano, "I'm Your Man," *Rockdelux* (Spain), May 1988.

19. In Shelagh Rogers, "Radio Interview," originally broadcast on "Sounds like Canada," CBC, February 7, 2006.

20. In Zollo, "Leonard Cohen."

21. In Jurek, "The Prophet of Love."

22. In Manzano, "The Future," 1993.

23. In Zollo, "Leonard Cohen."

24. In j. poet, "Happy at Last: The Poet Returns from His Zen Retreat with a New Album and a Sunnier Disposition," *Pulse!* November 2001.

25. In Sylvie Simmons, "Bringing It All Back Home," *Mojo,* March 2012.

26. In Sylvie Simmons, "Bringing It All Back Home."

27. In Dorian Lynskey, "All I've Got to Put in a Song Is My Own Experience," *Guardian,* January 19, 2012, theguardian.com/music/2012/jan/19/leonard-cohen.

28. In Alan Light, "Patti Smith Is (Still) Doing the Work," *Esquire,* March 10, 2022, esquire.com/entertainment/books/a39383363/patti-smith-melting-interview.

29. In Zollo, "Leonard Cohen."

30. In Paul Williams, "Leonard Cohen: The Romantic in a Ragpicker's Trade," *Crawdaddy!* March 1975.

# THE DRUNK IS GENDER-FREE

**(1)**
This morning I woke up again *(G D)*

I thank my Lord for that *(G D)*

The world is such a pigpen *(G/B   Am6)*

That I have to wear a hat *(G D)*

**(2)**
I love the Lord I praise the Lord *(C   G/C)*

I do the Lord forgive *(Am6)*

I hope I won't be sorry

For allowing Him to live

**(8)**
I know you like to get me drunk *(G D)*

And laugh at what I say *(G D)*

I'm very happy that you do

I'm thirsty   every day *(G D)*

**(3)**
I'm angry with the angel *(C   G)*

Who pinched me on the thigh *(D   G G7)*

And made me fall in love *(C C# D t)*

With every woman passing by *(Bb7   A7   G D G7)*

**(4)**
I know they are your sisters

Your daughters mothers wives

If I have left a woman out

Then I apologize

**C#**
It's fun to run|to heaven | *(C   G/B)*

When you're off the beaten| track *(Am6   G)*

The Lord is such a monkey

When you've got Him on your back

**(6)**
The Lord is such a monkey

He's such a woman too

Such a place of nothing

Such a face of you

**(6)**
May E crash into your temple

And look out thru' your eyes

And make you fall in love

With everybody you despise

1. This morning I woke up
2. I love the Lord
3. I'm angry w/the angel
4. I know they are your sisters
5. The Lord is such a monkey
6. May E Crash into your temple
7. This morning I woke up
8. I know you like to get me drunk

Fig. 1 Leonard Cohen, *You Can't Emerge*, 2003

# LEONARD COHEN'S SELF-PORTRAITS

## BETWEEN SKETCHES AND SCRAPBOOKING

Joan Angel

During his career, Leonard Cohen displayed hundreds of self-portraits through various modes of expression: photography, album covers, and sketches of his face surrounded by his handwritten words, selfies, Polaroids in notebooks, and more. Besides being a poet, a novelist, and a singer, Cohen was a self-portraitist, because most of his creations are centred on himself or his life experiences, and even when he speaks to or about others, or directly to God, he always portrays himself in the picture. When I reference self-portraits, I also include the literary ones, because self-representations can be made from all media: movies, books, performances, artifacts, installations. Anything can be used to represent someone, and the result may be a metaphor, an avatar, a tale, a kaleidoscopic vision, or a mosaicked version of the self with several traits blending.

Cohen knew that secret and exploited it by constantly reinventing himself in his self-portraits. Classifying self-portraiture as a genre is an intricate task, because each creation is meant to represent a unique individual in time, with an unprecedented form. Since the essence of the artform is based on creative processes through which an individual conceals an unpredictable statement within the final piece, self-portraiture defies genre.[1]

When reflecting on Cohen's possible statements in his self-portraits, I favour the two media that stand closest to his persona and private topics: sketches with handwritten comments and snapshots composed in notebooks. If the selfie catches moments of daily intimacy and could lead to insights about self-portraiture, I will leave the somewhat invasive phenomenon to studies that

one of those days
when the hat doesn't help

Fig. 2 Leonard Cohen, *One of Those Days*, 1980–1985

investigate the social pressure made on people regarding self-representation on social networks and in society.[2] As for Cohen's album covers, they certainly carry the spirit of each album, and Cohen's meaningful self-representations on them are worth noting,[3] but album covers follow the trends of the music industry, and in that sense, they represent a bias to intimacy or personal creativity. Cohen's sketches on which he drops a few lines of text, and the practice of scrapbooking with photographs and text, however, reveal idiosyncrasies that appear to be more insightful than stereotypical. Comments on sketches illustrate Cohen's daily moods and draw the lines of a personal diary. When a self-portrait becomes literary, such as when Cohen writes text alongside a representation of his face, the creative process is about "lining out" words and portraits together. And to appreciate Cohen's scrapbooking, I'll show how the writer, as public persona, edits several snapshots on one page (some with text), and why those pieces are self-portraits composed of different actions, such as profiling, addressing, and framing. The compositions hold an interest for those, like me, who seek to define the core of self-portraiture and its creative processes at work.

## Sketches and Scattered Words: Lining Out Moods

When artists repeat the old recipes that first granted them success and don't renew their repertoire of cultural artifacts—no matter the medium of expression they use—they become a caricature of themselves. In Cohen's numerous self-portraits in the books *The Flame* and *Book of Longing*, and even in his archive, he repeatedly caricatured his face; but not only that, he reinvented his own caricature through an exploration of the lines as he drew and redrew images of his face looking depressed. Mostly, the words reinvent the moods of his drawings.

In *You Can't Emerge* (fig. 1), Cohen's face is partially immersed in the environment of contrasting rectangles and squares. Emerging is contrary to immersing, and Cohen is likely referring to his face coming to the surface, but not quite as completely as he wishes. As such, the image and words together suggest moving through and coming out of something unknown and unnamed (abstract surroundings). The black markings draw the main caricature of Cohen's features with an expression of sadness, stained with torments in his crooked eyes. When viewed as a caricature, the portrait conveys a feeling of struggle that is comparable to the crisis artists go through in their careers. Whether famous, unknown, or infamous, an artist is dedicated to an artform or a craft, and therefore will have some experiences of failure and moments of stagnation that will feel like they're plunging into the void. Most artists will see themselves becoming vulnerable to disappearance; their art will die if they don't fight back. But if they do, they will thrive with greater creativity. In the moment this piece was created, perhaps Cohen could not see his victory beyond the battle.

The grey surfaces give a sense of solidity, adding drama to the picture: the forehead, skull, nose, and a few broken contours seem to stand against the colourful background. While the black markings define the features as a caricature, the patches of grey express resistance, the will to fight the eventual assimilation. There is another aspect to consider: Cohen suffered from chronic depression (*feeling grey*), which could explain the leitmotif of this work. Finally, the mouth remains an unfinished, open form as its outline crosses the contours of the face, pointing downward, and the literary input beside the face describes the mood. The skin-coloured lips emphasize a sulking expression, showing an undesired resilience rather than an attempt to counteract those invasive colours painting the face like a tapestry. Powerlessness is the main message, the image suggesting a gradual loss of Cohen's face. Maybe Cohen meant to criticize his own drawing by being dissatisfied with it. So, he would perceive himself as a low-class artist who cannot thrive with his original ideas or preconceived notions of what is "worth it" in visual art. Cohen was very fond of traditional Zen painting such as Zenga art[4] and, somehow, expressionism.[5] Improvisation played a big part in Cohen's creative process in painting; he probably made sense of the picture at the very end by adding a final line: "you can't emerge."

In the next picture (fig. 2), Cohen writes: "One of those days when the hat doesn't help." Unlike the previous image's dramatic tone, Cohen's self-deprecating sense of humour lightens up the spirit of this self-portrait. The hat is one of Cohen's signature objects, like the cigarette in hand, shiny shoes, and classy suits; the reoccurrences of these hallmarks became synonymous with Cohen's personal traits. Although, in this self-portrait, the writer brings new meaning to his hat as he reveals one of its flaws on "one of those days." What needs help? The sad morphology of those feminine lips coloured in pink (more definite here than in the previous portrait)? Is it that the hat won't help the mood of the day, nor the outfit perfectly matching the green, startled eyes? What did the hat usually make right that went wrong that day? We will never know. One thing that seems to be obvious, however, is the creative process: Cohen drew the lines of an anxious self-portrait that slid into the line of a joke—whether the subject was worrying about his look or his mood.

## Scrapbooking with Polaroids in Notebooks

The next self-portraits are composed of Polaroid snapshots assembled on notebook pages, a form of scrapbooking typical of Cohen, but not quite unique. Although the term "scrapbooking" appeared in the 1980s, the practice of pairing flat objects and/or photographs with commentary is a few centuries old. Such ornamented pages, bundled in a book or stashed in a box, are meant to become archives that remind the scrapbooker of special events or objects that hold sentimental value. As for the Polaroid cameras, they were commercialized in 1948. The two following pictures are dated from 1968, a pivotal year for Western cultures in terms of individual expression, the rise of social causes, new freedoms around sexual experiences, and the avalanche of artistic movements. In these explorative times, Cohen combines scrapbooking and Polaroid snapshots to create self-portraits that hint about their basic creative processes.

Profiling and Addressing

This collage entitled *Self-Portraits and Cut-Out* (fig. 3), reveals what inspired Cohen's album *Songs from a Room* (1969). The first Polaroid snapshot portrays Cohen as a writer by staging his desk, atop which a scarf is strewn across piles of scattered books, and a mocked-up album with no apparent title leans against the wall. The second snapshot zooms in on the album cover. The title, now visible, is unexpected: "Songs from My Room," rather than the album's "a room." Because Cohen's fans knew of his peripatetic lifestyle, and that he wrote from any hotel room he found himself in, "Songs from My Room," offers insight into Cohen's point of view on his writing. Wherever he was, Cohen made any room he wrote from his own. The final album cover hid that detail, so only the scrapbook page confirms this, but it also showcases one version of the process inside Cohen's private room. He also had a fetishized hotel room in New York to which he returned over and over. Cohen even wrote a song titled after that room for his album *New Skin for the Old Ceremony* (1974). The song, "Chelsea Hotel #2," was a tribute to his encounter with Janis Joplin at the Chelsea Hotel (the first version was never recorded; it was performed live). That same room was basically his own. More than just an anonymous space, it had some of his history in its walls.

Like the second snapshot, the third takes a closer view of the cover demo. We see the flash reflecting on the glossy black-and-white surface framing Cohen's portrait, but no title is in sight. The last snapshot is a cliché with a flash directing a totally different light on Cohen's face, with artsy effects, inside a mirror frame. Most interesting, is the cut-out profile beside that last snapshot. The idea of profiling oneself as a social representation didn't have such entertainment value as it does on social networks today, neither was it a wide practice. But in 1968, people frequently posed sideways in photo dispenser machines. Cohen innovates a form that creates his self-portrait from profiling, all on one page, with a collage of five Polaroid images that includes a close-up of his face and a snapshot for his artsy input, his role, and a statement about his own

creation. He signs it with that cut-out profile at the bottom of the page. This page, more than others, has a visionary quality to its presentation of an unprecedented form in self-portraiture at that time, and one that portends the daily action of millions of people today who share selfies on social networks.

This second scrapbook page, entitled *Cohen Cut-Out* (fig. 4), is a literary self-portrait with excerpts of Cohen's poetry placed above and beneath a collage. The photograph of Cohen may have been taken by someone else, but the cut-out of his figure and the placement of a black photo corner on his back signify that the picture is a composed self-portrait, a literary one, since Cohen represents himself by framing his picture with the two texts. Both are addressed to others: the first to a lover who is rejecting him, with the last line an address to a third party who hears his insistent desire, his plea to be loved, while the second is a short phrase addressed to a group of poets who have been celebrated for their oeuvre, and so has Cohen. The excerpts refer to two of Cohen's books of poetry: the one above from *The Energy of Slaves*,[6] published in 1972; and the one that appears in the 2018 posthumous work *Book of Longing,* which features a different picture alongside his words on page 82 (fig. 5).[7] These addresses play two functions in Cohen's literary self-portrait. The words frame Cohen's silhouette to indicate that this is a portrait of a writer, and at the same time, they show his pre-published words in handwritten form. They are archives of the work in progress, hidden in modest notebooks. Those four stanzas would be part of his future repertoire. As we read the piece today, we know where those phrases belong, but in 1968, neither he nor we would have known their future purpose. Did Cohen already know in which book those words would be published, and did he have the titles and content in mind? Probably not. A published version is a definite form that has been fixed and that also conceals its creative processes. Cohen might never have published those words, but still, as an archive, the piece would remain, a self-portrait. What is worth paying attention to in those pictures are the details of Cohen's intimate work-in-progress of his writing. Both texts are addressed to others, and they demonstrate some of Cohen's traits—such as his attachment to the desire for women, or his obsession with one—and a life marker for his professional glory.

Framing

In this last photograph (fig. 6), Cohen's self-portrait is shown with a dimmed light that barely reveals his white goatee, but it still stands out as the multiple lines around the head bring a focus inside the mirror: the door behind him, the sunlight coming from a front window, the different angles of the walls, the room next to him that gives a slight vision of the world through another window, and

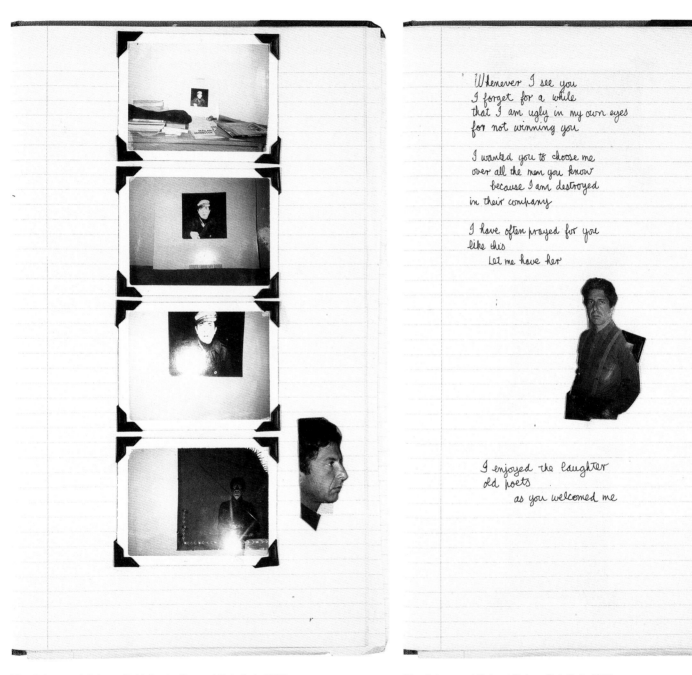

Whenever I see you
I forget for a while
that I am ugly in my own eyes
for not winning you

I wanted you to choose me
over all the men you know
      because I am destroyed
in their company

I have often prayed for you
like this
      Let me have her

I enjoyed the laughter
old poets
      as you welcomed me

Fig. 3 Leonard Cohen, *Self-Portraits and Cut-Out*, 1968

Fig. 4 Leonard Cohen, *Cohen Cut-Out*, 1968

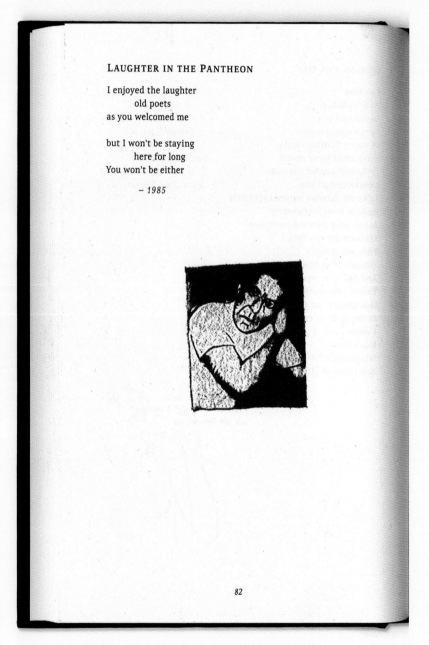

**LAUGHTER IN THE PANTHEON**

I enjoyed the laughter
        old poets
as you welcomed me

but I won't be staying
        here for long
You won't be either

        – 1985

*82*

Fig. 5 Leonard Cohen, Self-portrait in *Book of Longing*, 2006

Fig. 6 Leonard Cohen, *Desk*, 2000

the mirror frame that separates itself from an ensemble of artifacts displayed on top of the desk beneath it. In this case, "framing" seems to be the key to understanding the creative process in this composition. The mirroring of the persona with the perspective of different angles is the core of self-portraiture, with some surfaces lighter than others. Shadows may hide flaws, but the right level of luminosity also creates the perfect ambience for storytelling. The dimmed light contrasts a slight opening to the outside world in the back room—a statement that cautions against revealing secrets about oneself.

Although there are no words to accompany this picture, it is the self-portrait of a writer, rather than a literary self-portrait where anyone, not just writers, could describe themselves through literature. In that sense, what rests on top of the typing machine in the middle of the desk displays Cohen's idiosyncrasies as a writer: a notebook (works in progress), an open magazine (the writer's reading habits and culture), a pencil (the writer's main tool), and an unopened package (messages still unread or to be sent). The typing machine may be closed, but some work is still brewing on top of it. It portrays the mind of the writer, which is never at rest with its creative projects.

There is a telephone on the left side, not too dominant in the picture, like the small horizon in the back window, in contrast to the crooked lamp shade, which brings some movement into the picture. While something happened to it, we'll never know what, unless the self-portraitist wrote its story on the mirror. That simply didn't happen, but the image still suggests that the room's dweller didn't care to fix it, or simply chose to show it that way. This Polaroid is an excellent example of what I called earlier "a mosaicked version of the self," such as mirroring one's face, unravelling some secrets and composing personal traits from different angles and shades of light. Once the framing elements are in place, one must move beyond that phase because each self-portraitist cannot repeat somebody else's recipe; it would become a pastiche rather than a self-portrait. Thus, self-portraitists must devise a new form to describe their unique natures in time. It is only then that self-portraiture becomes an occasion to transform our crystallized caricatures.

—

JOAN ANGEL is a Canadian author who writes essays and novels. She has been an interdisciplinary artist since 1990. Her experience as a life model, art critic, painter, and makeup artist has influenced different forms of self-representation in literature. Leonard Cohen's self-portraiture has been one of her most inspiring subjects.

—

1. Since 2014, my research has focused on "intimate writings" of all kinds. The vast genre includes the subgenres of biography, memoir, autofiction, and self-portraiture (this list is not exhaustive).

2. See Tae Rang Choi, Yongjun Sung, Jung-Ah Lee, and Sejung Marina Choi, "Get behind My Selfies: The Big Five Traits and Social Networking Behaviors through Selfies," *Personality and Individual Differences* 109 (2017): 98–101, doi.org/10.1016/j.paid.2016.12.057; see also Nicola Bruno, Katarzyna Pisanski, Agnieszka Sorokowska, and Piotr Sorokowski, "Editorial: Understanding Selfies," *Frontiers in Psychology* 9, no. 44 (2018): https://doi.org/10.3389/fpsyg.2018.00044.

3. For an insightful study on Leonard Cohen's album covers, see Francis Mus, *The Demons of Leonard Cohen* (Ottawa: University of Ottawa Press, 2020).

4. On Zenga art, see Christophe Lebold, "Zen Drawings, Zen Humor: Leonard Cohen's Self Portraits as Spiritual Activators in *Book of Longing*," in *Book Practices and Textual Itineraries* 5, ed. Sophie Aymes, Brigitte Friant-Kessler, and Maxime Leroy (Nancy: PUN–Éditions Universitaires de Lorraine, 2017), 73–97.

5. See my chapter on Leonard Cohen's self-portraits: "The Humble One: A Polyptych of Self-Portraits in *Book of Longing* and *The Flame*," in *The Contemporary Leonard Cohen*, ed. Kait Pinder and Joel Deshaye (Waterloo: Wilfrid-Laurier University Press, forthcoming).

6. Leonard Cohen, *The Energy of Slaves* (Toronto: McClelland & Stewart, 1972).

7. Leonard Cohen, *Book of Longing* (Toronto: McClelland & Stewart, 2006).

Fig. 1 Leonard Cohen, *McCabe & Mrs. Miller*, 1971

# SEEKING FEELING

## LEONARD COHEN'S SONGS IN CINEMA

Laura Cameron and Jim Shedden

## Introduction

The opening scene of Robert Altman's 1971 film *McCabe & Mrs. Miller* (fig. 1) features a lone traveller on horseback winding his way slowly up a hill in the wilderness. He arrives at a small settlement—a crude clearing among the trees and rocks, some low shacks, a rustic church. People stare as he dismounts. He mutters a few words to himself but otherwise does not speak. Instead, Leonard Cohen's "The Stranger Song" wafts coolly across the landscape. The tension between Cohen's insistent fingerpicking on the guitar and his crooning, pensive voice establishes the character's state of mind —caught somewhere between urgency and melancholy, between hope and cynicism—and the lyrics operate almost like a voiceover to set up the drama that will follow. "He was just some Joseph looking for a manger," Cohen repeats as the lone figure, McCabe

(Warren Beatty), plods into town and makes his way to the ramshackle hotel; "He wants to trade the game he knows for shelter." Perhaps curiously, Altman added the song, along with two others from Cohen's first album, *Songs of Leonard Cohen* (1967), in post-production; but its mood and lyrics match the scene so perfectly that it seems as if the songs and script were written together. And while Cohen himself is nowhere to be seen on screen, his persona —dark, mysterious, rebellious, poetic—merges with McCabe's to create a composite character forged by music and cinema. Far from being an afterthought, the music is the heart of the film.

*McCabe & Mrs. Miller* was the first in a series of art films made in the 1970s that use Cohen's songs to establish atmosphere, worldview, theme, and character; Rainer Werner Fassbinder,

Fig. 2 Rainer Werner Fassbinder, *Beware of a Holy Whore,* 1971

Werner Herzog, and Bruce Elder, among others, drew from the Canadian singer-songwriter's oeuvre with similar enthusiasm. Foregrounding popular music in film without showing the singer on screen was, at the time, a recent innovation that originated famously with Mike Nichols's use of widely recognizable Simon & Garfunkel songs in *The Graduate* (1967). Previous filmmakers had used orchestral scores to varying effects in the background but incorporated popular music only when the musician was part of the scene—one might think of Elvis Presley singing in *Love Me Tender* (Robert D. Webb, 1956), for example, or Ricky Nelson and Dean Martin in *Rio Bravo* (Howard Hawks, 1959). When Nichols featured chart-topping hits like "The Sound of Silence" in *The Graduate,* however, the band was nowhere in sight, but the songs were intended to be heard, to be noticed. Although this approach seems familiar to us today, it represented an important shift in filmmaking in the late 1960s.

Leonard Cohen combined the earnest charm of Simon & Garfunkel and the political urgency of Bob Dylan with a unique blend of personas all his own—the countercultural rebel, the Jewish philosopher, the spiritual seeker, the unapologetic seducer. In 1971, when *McCabe* was released, the thirty-six-year-old Cohen was still relatively new to the music scene, though his first volume of poetry had come out more than a decade earlier, and he had published four others and two novels in the meantime. But the charismatic "son of Montreal" fast outgrew the burgeoning and yet still provincial poetry scene in Canada. When the National Film Board of Canada set out in 1964 to make a documentary about four poets —Earle Birney, Irving Layton, Phyllis Gotlieb, and Leonard Cohen— Cohen so outshone the others that they ended up making the film all about him, and it became the now-classic *Ladies and Gentlemen . . . Mr. Leonard Cohen* (1965). It features clips from a reading tour, and intimate but staged scenes from Cohen's "life" (long before reality TV): in one sequence, he takes a bath in his Montreal hotel room and then orders a sandwich; in another, he fools around charmingly on the harmonica as a late-night party comes to an end. When, a few years later, Cohen won a Governor General's Award for his 1968 *Selected Poems,* he turned it down because, as he wrote in a charmingly elusive telegram from Europe, "The poems themselves forbid it absolutely."[1] As opportunities in the music world multiplied, Cohen was beginning to forge the celebrity persona for which he would become known. He chased contradiction and relentlessly pursued enigma. Cohen was a cool intellectual, a bourgeois gentleman, an intimate exhibitionist, a popular outsider.

When filmmakers use his music in their movies, they import those personas, to varying degrees, along with the melody and lyrics. This essay can only touch upon some of the films that feature Cohen's songs, but our goal is to draw out a few commonalities to offer some sense of the role his music plays in cinema—of what

makes it "cinematic." We focus mainly on those early films, but there has been a resurgence of interest in Cohen's music in recent years: just as Cohen moved from the fringes of popular culture into the mainstream, so too did his music. Blockbuster Hollywood productions like the TV series *True Detective* (2014 to 2019) and, perhaps best known of all, the movie *Shrek* (Andrew Adamson, Vicky Jenson, 2001) have used his songs. But while the genres of film might have changed and Cohen's own cocktail of personas has been remixed over the years, the effect of his music in films has remained relatively stable: whether the lyrics support the narrative by serving as a kind of voiceover, as in *McCabe & Mrs. Miller,* or whether the music simply offers an aural counterpoint to poetic imagery, Cohen's songs tend to work against the linear medium of film, creating meditative pockets of time, mood, and emotion even as the "moving picture" itself runs on.

The 1970s: Fassbinder, Herzog, Elder

No one incorporated more Cohen songs into his films than the German filmmaker Rainer Werner Fassbinder. In *Beware of a Holy Whore* (1971) (fig. 2), a self-referential film about filmmaking, six Cohen songs play on a jukebox, along with selections by Elvis Presley, Ray Charles, and Spooky Tooth. The jukebox is situated in the lobby of a seaside hotel in Spain, where the cast and crew of a film are milling about, waiting for their production money to come through, and obsessing about the power dynamics among themselves in the meantime. *Beware of a Holy Whore* is all about biding time, and about the anxious and claustrophobic inertia that can be involved in the artistic process—both the mundane stuck-ness of waiting for people and money, and the grander, more enigmatic, stasis of waiting for inspiration. Cohen's music, meanwhile, creates a different kind of stillness that heightens the tension through contrast. While the film crew is exiled in the hotel lobby, their progress hampered by acrimonious infighting and the vagaries of the film industry, the songs offer a contemplative stillness, a "seeking" that feels pure rather than petty. The cacophony of the scene drives the juxtaposition home on a visceral level; there is a fruitful disjunction between, as Margaret Barton-Fumo puts it, the impetuous yells of the film's high-strung producer (played by Fassbinder himself) and Cohen's "undulating baritone."[2] Not only that, but Fassbinder's audiences in Europe, where Cohen was already wildly popular in 1971 (though his fame had not yet skyrocketed in America), would have associated his voice with dark intellectualism and spiritual searching—that is, with the complex persona he was cultivating. The expansive stillness of the lyric mode works against the anxious stasis that Fassbinder portrays on screen.

Whereas for Fassbinder, Cohen's songs seem to offer refuge from the inexorable demands of narrative logic while still allowing the story to develop, Werner Herzog's juxtaposition of music and imagery in *Fata Morgana* (1971) purposefully defies meaning. Cohen's "Suzanne" and "So Long, Marianne" play one after the other as the camera tracks fluidly from left to right across the Sahara Desert. Mesmerizing footage of mirages, small roads, fences, huts, and warehouses runs on, almost like a series of still images, and over it all Cohen sings of longing and love. The barren imagery, understood in the context of Herzog's own comment that this was a film about colonialism, evokes both an ending and a beginning—a place in ruins, one that has been emptied out, and a new place, empty and waiting to be filled. And even for viewers who do not understand the English lyrics (the voiceover narration, done by Herzog himself, is in German), the sweeping crescendos of the choruses, creates an impression of rolling hills, an aural plane that contrasts with the flat desert landscape. Similarly, the continuous panning shots operate horizontally, while the expression of the individual lyric voice operates vertically, capturing a single feeling in all its multiple dimensions. The scenery is desolate and the camera work monotonous; but the songs are so full, their rhythms and swells pulsing with life, that they demand our attention. There might be a thematic relationship between image and sound, or they might simply create a contemplative counterpoint, two tracks running in parallel, the closest cinema can take us to a daydream.

At the other end of the 1970s, the Canadian filmmaker and scholar Bruce Elder incorporated Cohen's "Teachers" to similar effect in *The Art of Worldly Wisdom* (1979), an autobiographical film from the start of his *Book of All the Dead* cycle. Elder splintered Herzog's contrapuntal technique, running multiple soundtracks and image tracks in competition with one another to create a visually and aurally polyphonic effect. And yet here, the lyrics are definitely harmonious with the theme of the film: both are about seeking at a moment of personal crisis—recalling, explicitly in the film's case, Dante at the beginning of *The Divine Comedy*. Cohen's "Teachers," also from *Songs of Leonard Cohen*, focuses on a young artist's coming to voice. The singer faces two paths and worries that they cannot co-exist: either he embraces the ascetic life of the artist or he embraces life's pleasures—food andwomen— and sacrifices the purity of his art. Elder and Cohen were both in their early thirties when they made these works, and their similar expression of crisis and confusion might reflect a certain stage of adulthood. The polyphony of the film, which forces the viewer to engage with it at a macromorphological level, taking in the whole thing rather than understanding each of its constituent parts, in some ways embodies the overwhelming experience of anxiety or depression; Cohen's lyrics, too, evoke the claustrophobia of trying to choose the right path. Both works express or at least meditate on the paralysis of creative crisis.

## The 1990s and Beyond: Cohen's New Cool

While Cohen's reputation arguably slumped in the 1980s—his album *Various Positions* was largely dismissed when it was released in 1984—several songs from his 1992 album *The Future* feature in Oliver Stone's 1994 film *Natural Born Killers* (fig. 3), part of a super-cool soundtrack assembled by Trent Reznor (of Nine Inch Nails) that reinforced Cohen's continuing relevance in the 1990s. Unlike Herzog, Stone self-consciously engages Cohen's music to convey the message of the film. The protagonists, Mickey and Mallory Knox (Woody Harrelson and Juliette Lewis), are criminals engaged in a ruthless killing spree throughout the movie. After they commit their final murder, Stone runs a sequence of real television news clips depicting violent events from the era, offering a bitter comment on the way in which the media glorifies horrific violence. Then the credits roll, with Cohen's "The Future" playing over a montage of earlier scenes from the movie, as well as images of Mickey and Mallory's "happily ever after" life, apparently free at last from crime. The lyrics of "The Future" are some of Cohen's most explicitly political: the final lines are "Give me back the Berlin Wall, / Give me Stalin and St. Paul, / I've seen the future, brother / It is murder." By playing this song about the inevitability of murder over "happily ever after" images, and by playing a song about the "future" over scenes from the "past," Stone creates an ironic trap that closes the film in on itself—insisting, as the song does, that history repeats itself, that our ending is in our beginning. As in the Altman, Fassbinder, and Herzog films, in *Natural Born Killers* Cohen's music stops linear progress, though it does so not by adding a "vertical" emotional dimension to "horizontal" narrative time but by simply denying the possibility of ending (or of ending violence)—a denial that the lyrics and the movie both endorse.

The lyrics also support the narrative in what might be the best-known example of Cohen's music in cinema: John Cale's cover of "Hallelujah" in *Shrek* (fig. 4). As in *McCabe & Mrs. Miller*, the song offers a kind of voiceover in *Shrek*, running on top of the visual imagery to express the character's innermost feelings; and as in *Beware of a Holy Whore* and *Fata Morgana*, the music works against the linear progress of the narrative and imagery, slowing the story to insist on self-reflection. Near the end of the film, a misunderstanding provokes Shrek (Mike Myers) to renounce both Princess Fiona (Cameron Diaz) and his best friend, Donkey (Eddie Murphy). "Hallelujah" plays as Shrek returns home to the solitude of his swamp and Fiona prepares to marry the odious Lord Farquaad (John Lithgow). Both Shrek and Fiona are lonely and regretful, and some of the lyrics quite unambiguously express Shrek's feelings in the moment: "I used to live alone before I knew you"—indeed. Crucially, the song intervenes when the conflict has reached a fever pitch and the narrative cannot progress any further without

Fig. 3 Oliver Stone, *Natural Born Killers*, 1994

Fig. 4 Andrew Adamson and Vicky Jenson, *Shrek*, 2001

Fig. 5 Sarah Polley, *Take This Waltz*, 2011

a spiritual or emotional reckoning. In this way, the song, almost like a *deus ex machina*—the Greek theatrical device that magically resolves the drama before the play's conclusion—does what the dialogue, action, and mise en scène of film cannot: it makes space for feeling and holds us there with the characters. As Alan Light writes, the song's "sorrowful but unsentimental tone fit the sophistication of [the cartoon]."[3] *Shrek,* like "Hallelujah" and, like Cohen, embodies contradictions—the kindly ogre, the monastic ladies' man; the sophisticated cartoon, the unsentimental sorrow.

The presence of Cohen's songs in cinema increased exponentially after *Shrek,* which was the top-grossing film of 2001 and which catapulted Cohen's music (if not Cohen himself) to fame in the eyes of a new generation. "Hallelujah" now signifies emotional reckoning to listeners across the world, and filmmakers have come to trust that other songs—"Take This Waltz," "Bird on the Wire," and "Dance Me to the End of Love," among others—will also be quickly recognizable to a wide audience. In Sarah Polley's *Take This Waltz* (2011) (fig. 5), Feist's cover of "Closing Time" plays over a warm and erotically charged party scene. And in the second season of *True Detective* (2015) (fig. 6), the more recent song "Nevermind" is layered over the visually arresting opening credits, cut so that different parts of the song and different lyrics are featured in each episode.

The cinematic appeal of Cohen's music might lie in the atmosphere of its rhythms, jaunty or plodding or smooth, or in the emotional expressiveness of the lyrics. It might lie in the characters the songs create—Suzanne, Marianne—or in the character of Cohen himself, which shifted shapes so many times over his long career—Jewish Montrealer, poet, folk crooner, pop star, saint, "a sportsman and a shepherd, / . . . a lazy bastard living in a suit"—and continues to metamorphose today, even as his death recedes into the past. His distinctive voice, once reedy, by the end faded to a gravelly whisper, can stand in for the filmmaker's consciousness or a character's inner thoughts. The director Matt Bissonnette, speaking about his 2020 film *Death of a Ladies' Man,* proposed that the songs are themselves "actually a character"[4]—and certainly much more than background music. Sometimes, too, they are stories of their own: they operate like mini-narratives nested within the larger narrative of the film, intertexts that have their own independent existence, and that change or are changed by the images on the screen. The films we have discussed here diverge wildly in subject matter and approach, taking us from the barren Sahara of *Fata Morgana* to the animated swamp of *Shrek,* and yet in all cases Cohen's songs create an emotional or contemplative space, a kind of refuge (or trap, in *Natural Born Killers*), for filmmaker and viewer alike, from the linear time and narrative logic of the film. They are instantly familiar, impossibly cool, and always, as the poet put it himself in "Famous Blue Raincoat," "Sincerely, L Cohen."

LAURA CAMERON holds a PhD in English from McGill University, where she wrote about the creative careers of twentieth-century Canadian poets such as P.K. Page and Leonard Cohen. She was previously the Assistant Editor of Publications & Exhibitions at the Art Gallery of Ontario before going on to study law at the University of Toronto.

JIM SHEDDEN is responsible for the publishing program at the Art Gallery of Ontario, where he has also curated interdisciplinary exhibitions, including *I AM HERE: Home Movies and Everyday Masterpieces* and *Guillermo del Toro: At Home with Monsters.* Shedden was the Vice-President and a creative producer at Bruce Mau Design from 1998 to 2010. He recently co-edited *Moments of Perception: Experimental Film in Canada,* and has directed a number of films on music and art.

1. In Michael Posner, *Leonard Cohen, Untold Stories,* vol. 1, *The Early Years* (Toronto: Simon & Schuster, 2020), 415.

2. Margaret Barton-Fumo, "Deep Cuts: Leonard Cohen," *Film Comment,* February 6, 2017, filmcomment.com/blog/deep-cuts-leonard-cohen/.

3. Alan Light, *The Holy or the Broken: Leonard Cohen, Jeff Buckley, and the Unlikely Ascent of "Hallelujah"* (New York: Atria Books, 2012), 100.

4. Brad Wheeler, "Matthew Bissonnette on His Love for Leonard Cohen's Music, and Its Role in His New Film *Death of a Ladies' Man,*" *Globe and Mail,* March 11, 2021, theglobeandmail.com/arts/film/reviews/article-matthew-bissonnette-on-his-love-for-leonard-cohens-music-and-its-role/.

With long-time collaborator Patrick Leonard and his son, Adam, Cohen did much of the work for his last album, *You Want It Darker* (2016), from a medical chair in the living room of his Los Angeles home. The album was released just three weeks before his death, Cohen left his son with instructions to finish the songs they'd started together. Adam wrote and recorded arrangements for each as he believed his father would have wanted to hear them. The result is *Thanks for the Dance*, a posthumous album of previously unreleased material that's a fitting cap to Cohen's distinguished career as a recording artist.

The album features a number of previous collaborators and music world notables, from Anjani Thomas—who wrote the music for the title track and convinced Cohen to complete the lyrics—to Sharon Robinson, Jennifer Warnes, Patrick Watson, Damien Rice, Leslie Feist, Daniel Lanois, and many others. The last poem Cohen ever recorded, "Listen to the Hummingbird," is a surrender to mortality and the vast world beyond:

> Listen to the hummingbird
> Whose wings you cannot see
> Listen to the hummingbird
> Don't listen to me
> Listen to the butterfly
> Whose days but number three
> Listen to the butterfly
> Don't listen to me
> Listen to the mind of God
> Which doesn't need to be
> Listen to the mind of God
> Don't listen to me
> Listen to the hummingbird
> Whose wings you cannot see
> Listen to the hummingbird
> Don't listen to me

Leonard Cohen,
*Thanks for the Dance*,
2019

Leonard Cohen,
*You Want It Darker*,
2016

The final collection of Cohen's late poems, lyrics, prose pieces, drawings, and notebook excerpts, *The Flame* demonstrates that Cohen's lyricism continued through his final days, as did his characteristic humour.

In 2022, Leonard Cohen's never-before published fiction was compiled into a new volume titled *A Ballet of Lepers: A Novel and Stories.* The book's contents were written between 1956 and 1961.

Leonard Cohen, *The Flame,* 2018

Leonard Cohen, *A Ballet of Lepers,* 2022

Kara Blake, *The Offerings*, 2017

Commissioned by Musée d'art contemporain de Montréal,
*The Offerings* provides an exploration of Leonard Cohen's mind
through an immersive visual experience in his own words.
Drawn from a wealth of archival sources, Kara Blake uses excerpts
from Cohen's interviews and recordings to reveal his artistic
preferences. She constructs a composite portrait of the artist as he
touches on a variety of subjects, ranging from his personal writing
practice to universal themes of love, humility, and spirituality.

George Fok, *Passing Through*, 2017

The immersive video work *Passing Through* celebrates Cohen's singular voice, music, charismatic persona, and inimitable stage presence. Drawing on a vast archive of audiovisual material, George Fok pays tribute to Cohen's monumental, five-decade career as a singer-songwriter and performer. This composite portrait of Cohen recalls and reconstructs various pivotal stages in his career, from his early years in bohemian 1960s Montreal to his later life, when he was recognized as a global cultural icon.

The audience time travels through a collage of collective memories, musical moments, and emotions that have enchanted generations of fans around the world.

To honour the contribution that Leonard
Cohen made to the city's culture, MU,
a not-for-profit organization, commissioned
Montreal artist Gene Pendon and interna-
tionally renowned American street artist
El Mac to create a 10,000-square-foot mural
rising twenty-one storeys above the city
of Montreal. Pendon, El Mac, and their team
replicated a photograph taken by Cohen's
daughter, Lorca. The mural quickly became
a spectacular visual landmark and an icon in
the city of Montreal.

Gene Pendon and El Mac, *Tower of Songs,* 2017

*Beautiful Losers*
1966
Book
21.6 × 14 cm
Thomas Fisher Rare Book Library,
University of Toronto
Page 39

*Beautiful Losers*
1970
Book
22 × 14 cm
Thomas Fisher Rare Book Library,
University of Toronto
Page 39

*Beautiful Losers*
1972
Book
22 × 14 cm
Thomas Fisher Rare Book Library,
University of Toronto
Page 39

*Beautiful Losers*
1976
Book
17.6 × 10.7 cm
Thomas Fisher Rare Book Library,
University of Toronto
Page 39

*Beautiful Losers*
1986
Book
17.6 × 10.7 cm
Thomas Fisher Rare Book Library,
University of Toronto
Page 39

*Beautiful Losers*
1991
Book
17.6 × 10.7 cm
Thomas Fisher Rare Book Library,
University of Toronto
Page 39

Judy Collins
*In My Life*
1966
Album cover
31.4 × 31.4 cm
Page 40

Mariposa Folk Festival poster
1967
Ink on paper
Dimensions unknown
Page 40

*Songs of Leonard Cohen*
1967
Album cover
31.4 × 31.4 cm
Page 41

CBS Records press release
1968
Ink on bond paper
25 × 20 cm
Page 41

*Max's Kansas City*
1967
Inscription on printed menu
Overall: 18.6 × 26.2 cm
Page 42

*Selected Poems, 1956–1968*
1968
Book
20.3 × 14 cm
Thomas Fisher Rare Book Library,
University of Toronto
Page 43

*Tennessee Notebook* cover
1968
Notebook
33 × 21 cm
Page 44

*View from Window*
1968
Notebook with Polaroid Type 20
instant prints
Overall: 31.8 × 19.7 cm
Page 45

*Forlorn Harvest*
1968
Notebook with Polaroid Type 20
instant prints
Overall: 31.8 × 19.7 cm
Page 45

*Death After Death*
1968
Notebook with Polaroid Type 20
instant prints
Overall: 31.8 × 19.7 cm
Page 46

*Desk in Room 1219*
1968
Notebook with Polaroid Type 20
instant prints
Overall: 31.8 × 19.7 cm
Images: 6.4 × 8.3 cm
and 8.3 × 6.4 cm each
Page 47

*6 am False Faces*
1968
Notebook with Polaroid Type 20
instant prints
Overall: 31.8 × 19.7 cm
Image: 8.3 × 6.4 cm each
Page 48

*Self-Portraits and Cut-Out*
1968
Notebook with Polaroid Type 2
instant prints
Overall: 31.8 × 19.7 cm
Image: 8.3 × 6.4 cm each
Page 49

*She Yawned*
1968
Notebook with Polaroid Type 20
instant prints
Overall: 31.8 × 19.7 cm
Image: 8.3 × 6.4 cm
Page 49

*Cohen Cut-Out*
1968
Notebook with Polaroid Type 20
instant prints
Overall: 31.8 × 19.7 cm
Image: 8.3 × 6.4 cm
Page 50

*Nude Torso*
1968–1969
Notebook with Polaroid Type 20
instant prints
Overall: 31.8 × 19.7 cm
Image: 8.3 × 6.4 cm each
Page 51

*After and Before the Swim at the Y*
1968–1969
Notebook with Polaroid Type 20
instant prints
Overall: 31.8 × 19.7 cm
Page 51

*Songs from a Room*
1969
Album cover
31.4 × 31.4 cm
Page 51

Murray Lerner
*Message to Love: The Isle of Wight
Festival, 1970*
1970
35mm and 16mm film
(colour, sound, 127 min.)
Page 52

*Leonard Cohen: Songs of Love
and Hate*
1971
Album cover
31.4 × 31.4 cm
Page 53

Suzanne Elrod
*Acapulco*
1971
Gelatin silver print
9.1 × 9.4 cm
Page 54

*The Energy of Slaves* back cover
1972
Book
22.5 × 14.5 cm
Ted East Collection
Page 54

*Leonard Cohen: Live Songs*
1973
Album cover
31.4 × 31.4 cm
Page 54

*Self-Portrait*
1979
Instant print (Polaroid Type 667)
8.3 × 10.8 cm
Page 55

*Self-Portrait*
1979
Instant print (Polaroid Type 667)
8.3 × 10.8 cm
Page 55

*Self-Portrait*
1979
Instant print (Polaroid Type 667)
8.3 × 10.8 cm
Page 55

Unknown maker
*Poet of Rock*
1972
Poster
59.7 × 82.6 cm
Page 56

Europe and Israel concert
tour footage
1972
Video scanned from 16mm film
(colour, sound, 6 min.)
Pages 56–57

*Self-Portrait II (Pastel Notebook)*
1980–1985
Pastel and crayon notebook
containing 16 drawings
33 × 23 cm
Page 69

Lynn Ball
*Leonard Cohen on Boulevard
Saint-Laurent, Montreal*
c. 1983
Chromogenic print
25.4 × 20.3 cm
Page 70

Lynn Ball
*Leonard Cohen on Boulevard
Saint-Laurent, Montreal*
c. 1983
Chromogenic print
Overall: 20.3 × 25.4 cm
Page 71

Unknown photographer
*Adam Cohen*
c. 1975
Gelatin silver print
6.03 × 5.87 cm
Page 72

Unknown photographer
*Lorca Cohen*
c. 1980
Gelatin silver print
12.7 × 17.78 cm
Page 72

*Lorca, Leonard, and
Adam Cohen Photo Booth Strip*
1978
Gelatin silver print
20.5 × 5 cm
Courtesy of the artist
Page 73

Unknown photographer
*Cohen at Home in Montreal*
1975–1980
Gelatin silver print
25.4 × 20.3 cm
Page 73

Unknown photographer
*Adam Cohen, Suzanne Elrod,
Leonard Cohen, and Masha Cohen
in Montreal*
1972
Gelatin silver print
Dimensions unknown
Page 73

Unknown photographer
*Leonard Cohen*
c. 1979
Gelatin silver print
Dimensions unknown
Page 74

*I Am a Hotel*
1983
TV short musical film,
frame enlargement
(colour, sound, 28 min.)
Written by Leonard Cohen
and Mark Shekter, directed
by Allan F. Nicholls
Page 74

*Greatest Hits*
1975
Album cover
31.4 × 31.4 cm
Page 75

*Death of a Ladies' Man*
1977
Album cover
31.4 × 31.4 cm
Page 75

*Recent Songs*
1979
Album cover
31.4 × 31.4 cm
Page 75

*Field Commander Cohen:
Tour of 1979*
2001
Album cover
31.4 × 31.4 cm
Page 75

Unknown photographer
*Leonard Cohen in Montreal*
c. 1975
Gelatin silver print
Dimensions unknown
Page 76

Harry Rasky
*The Song of Leonard Cohen*
1980
16mm film made for CBC Television,
frame enlargement (colour, sound,
90 min.)
Page 76

Unknown photographer
*Leonard Cohen in Hydra*
c. 1974
Gelatin silver print
Dimensions unknown
Page 76

"The Event" (*1972 Notebook*)
1972
Published in *Death of a Lady's Man*
(1978)
Ink on paper
9.5 × 6 cm
Page 77

"Death of a Lady's Man" (*1973 Hydra
Notebook*)
1973
Published in *Death of a Lady's Man*
(1978)
Ink on paper
12.7 × 8.9 cm
Page 77

Lynn Ball
*Contact Sheet*
c. 1985
Chromogenic print
25.4 × 20.3 cm
Pages 78–79

*Self-Portrait: Various Positions,
Outtake 1*
1984
Instant print (Polaroid Type 600)
7.9 × 7.9 cm
Page 80

*Self-Portrait: Various Positions,
Outtake 2*
1984
Instant print (Polaroid Type 600)
7.9 × 7.9 cm
Page 80

*Self-Portrait: Various Positions,
Outtake 3*
1984
Instant print (Polaroid Type 600)
7.9 × 7.9 cm
Page 80

*Various Positions*
1984
Album cover
31.4 × 31.4 cm
Page 80

"Hallelujah"
Words and music by Leonard Cohen
1979–1984
Song sheet
31.1 × 96.5 cm
© 1984 Sony / ATV Songs, LLC /
Stranger Music, Inc. /
Hipgnosis Songs
Page 81

Richard McCaffrey
*Leonard Cohen and Jennifer Warnes
with Sharon Robinson and Mitch
Watkins perform live at the Greek
Theatre in Berkeley, California*
1983
Gelatin silver print
Dimensions unknown
© Richard McCaffrey / Michael Ochs
Archive via Getty Images
Page 82

Jennifer Warnes
*Famous Blue Raincoat*
1986
Album cover
31.4 × 31.4 cm
Page 83

"There Was a Child Named
Bernadette II"
1986
Handwritten poem
21.2 × 16.3 cm
Page 83

"There Was a Child Named
Bernadette"
1986
Handwritten poem
21.2 × 16.3 cm
Page 83

"First We Take Manhattan"
1986
Typed page
28.7 × 22.5 cm
Page 84

"First We Take Manhattan II"
1986
Typed page
28.7 × 22.5 cm
Page 84

*Leonard Cohen: I'm Your Man*
1988
CD album cover
12 × 12 cm
Courtesy of Kristina Ljubanovic
Page 85

*Popular Problems*
2014
Album cover
31.4 × 31.4 cm
Page 102

Kezban Ozcan
*Leonard Cohen and Patrick Leonard*
c. 2013
Digital photograph
Page 103

*Anjani*
2000
Instant print (Polaroid Type 600)
9.2 × 7.9 cm
Page 103

Unified Heart
Scan from *Book of Mercy* (1984)
Page 104

*Leonard Cohen: The Future
World Tour* leather jacket
1993
Dimensions unknown
Page 106

*Cohen's Desk* (Los Angeles)
1991
Instant print (Polaroid Spectra)
10.1 × 10.3 cm
Page 108

*Cohen Live*
1994
Album cover
31.4 × 31.4 cm
Page 108

*Dear Heather*
2004
Album cover
31.4 × 31.4 cm
Page 110

"Go No More A-Rovin'" lyrics
in *Dear Heather*
2004
CD album art
12 × 12 cm
Page 110

Drawings in *Book of Longing*
2006
Ink on paper
23 × 15 cm
Page 110

Philip Glass
*Book of Longing*
2007
CD album cover
12 × 12 cm
Page 110

*Green Chair*
2011
Inkjet, edition 90/100
38.1 × 30.5 cm
Page 112

*My Mother's Last Hand
(Watercolour Notebook)*
1980–1985
Watercolour notebook containing
13 watercolours
21.1 × 35 cm
Page 112

Scrim projection of Leonard
Cohen's *Woman and Horse*
(1980–1985) during his world
tour concert in Berlin
2013
Digital photograph
Photo © Uwe Schrade
Page 114

Leonard Cohen and Michael Petit
*Leonard Cohen: The Future
World Tour* t-shirt
1993
Courtesy of Michael Petit
Page 115

Leonard Cohen and Michael Petit
Concert merchandise
Assorted ephemera
Dimensions variable
1992–2008
Courtesy of Michael Petit
Pages 116–117

*Imperial Hotel Journal Entry*
1974
Notebook
Overall: 24.5 × 16.5 cm
Page 121

*"Hallelujah" Notebook*
1983–1984
Notebook
Overall: 23.5 × 19 cm
Page 122

"Everybody Knows"
1987
Notebook
22.7 × 17.5 cm
Page 124

"Anthem"
1991
Notebook
33 × 21 cm
Page 126

"The Drunk Is Gender-Free,"
2004
Printed page
27.9 × 21.6
Page 129

*You Can't Emerge*
2003
Digital drawing
Page 130

*One of Those Days*
1980–1985
Watercolour notebook
21.1 × 35 cm
Page 132

*Self-Portraits and Cut-Out*
1968
Notebook with Polaroid Type 20
instant prints
Overall: 31.8 × 19.7 cm
Page 135

*Cohen Cut-Out*
1968
Notebook with Polaroid Type 20
instant prints
Overall: 31.8 × 19.7 cm
Page 135

Self-portrait in *Book of Longing*
2006
Ink on paper
23 × 15 cm
Page 136

*Desk*
2000
Polaroid SX-70
7.9 × 7.9 cm
Page 136

*McCabe & Mrs. Miller*
1971
Album cover
31.4 × 31.4 cm
Page 138

Rainer Werner Fassbinder
*Beware of a Holy Whore*
1971
Film, frame enlargement
(colour, sound, 103 min.)
Page 140

Oliver Stone
*Natural Born Killers*
1994
Film, frame enlargement
(colour, sound, 109 min.)
Page 143

Andrew Adamson and Vicky Jenson
*Shrek*
2001
Computer-animated movie,
frame enlargement
(colour, sound, 90 min.)
Page 143

Sarah Polley
*Take This Waltz*
2011
Film, frame enlargement (colour,
sound, 116 min.)
Page 144

Nic Pizzolatto
*True Detective* (season two)
2015
TV show, frame enlargement
(colour, sound)
Page 144

*Thanks for the Dance*
2019
Album cover
31.4 × 31.4 cm
Page 146

*You Want It Darker*
2016
Album cover
31.4 × 31.4 cm
Page 146

*The Flame*
2018
Book
22.86 × 15.24 cm
Page 147

A Ballet of Lepers
2022
Book
23.62 × 15.75 cm
Page 147

Kara Blake
The Offerings
2017
Five-channel video installation
(black and white / colour, sound,
35 min.)
Installation view of the exhibition
Leonard Cohen: A Crack in
Everything, presented at the Musée
d'art contemporain de Montréal,
2017–2018
Courtesy of the artist and archival
images © University of Toronto
Libraries
Photo: Richard-Max Tremblay
Page 148

George Fok
Passing Through
2017
Multi-channel video installation
(black and white / colour, sound,
56 min. 15 sec.)
Installation view of the exhibition
Leonard Cohen: A Crack in
Everything, presented at the Musée
d'art contemporain de Montréal,
2017–2018
Courtesy of the artist
Photo: Guy L'Heureux
Page 149

Gene Pendon and El Mac
Tower of Songs
2017
Acrylic and spray paint
Lighting designer: Ombrages
Photo: Jean-François Savaria, 2019
Page 151

"With a Peacock's Feather"
Date unknown
Written poem
Overall: 27.9 × 21.6 cm
Page 166

Self-Portrait with Mirrored Glasses
2009
Crayon and ink on paper
Overall: 22.3 × 29 cm
Page 168

FRONT ENDPAPERS:

21-25
c.1985
23.5 × 15.88 cm

33-16
1960s
14.6 × 8.23 cm

44-16
Date unknown
12.1 × 7 cm

4-15
1965–1966
16.51 × 10.16 cm

22-16
1969
22.23 × 17.15 cm

20-16
1960
15.24 × 10.16 cm

30-25
c.1990
31.75 × 19.38 cm

4-17
1979
7.62 × 7 cm

36-16
1960s
11.43 × 7.24 cm

38-16
1960s
11.76 × 8.26 cm

1-16
c.1966
12.07 × 6.99 cm

Tennessee Notebook
1968
33 × 21 cm

33–16
1960s
14.6 × 8.26 cm

17-16
c.1968
17.78 × 11.43 cm

49-16
1960s–1970s
24.77 × 17.15 cm

18-16
1966
19.69 × 12.07 cm

32-16
1960s
13.97 × 8.59 cm

3-40
October 2005–July 2006
Dimensions unknown

21-16
1969
10.16 × 3.18 cm

14-16
c.1966
20.32 × 12.7 cm

43-16
1972
9.53 × 6.35 cm

16-16
c.1968
22.23 × 11.43 cm

26-16
1969
22.23 × 17.15 cm

——

BACK ENDPAPERS:

28-16
1973–1974
16.51 × 10.16 cm

4-45
2000–2006
17.78 × 12.7 cm

2-40
2008
14.61 × 10.49 cm

7-16
c.1962
13.97 × 7.62 cm

2-30
1970s–1980s
21.59 × 17.78 cm

28-16
1973–1974
16.51 × 10.16 cm

Guide to the Notebooks 2
1994
35.56 × 29.59 cm

Large Block
Date unknown
26.67 × 24.13 cm

45-16
1960s
12.07 × 6.99 cm

27-16
1973–1976
20.32 × 14.61 cm

12-16
c.1966
19.69 × 12.07 cm

15-25
1988
Dimensions unknown

7-45
1974
22.23 × 14.61 cm

6-45
2002–2003
18.42 × 12.7 cm

5-40
2013–2013
20.96 × 14.61 cm

37-16
1973
11.43 × 6.99 cm

9-15
c.1966
12.7 × 7.62 cm

3-45
Date unknown
12.7 × 7.62 cm

1-45
Date unknown
29.21 × 21.59 cm

32-16
1960s
13.97 × 8.59 cm

5-45
Date unknown
21.59 × 15.24 cm

INSIDE HIS ARCHIVE ENDNOTES

1. Nick Mount, *Arrival* (Toronto: House of Anansi Press, 2017), 206.

2. Sylvie Simmons, *I'm Your Man: The Life of Leonard Cohen* (Toronto: McClelland & Stewart, 2012), 119.

3. David and Lucy Boucher, *Bob Dylan and Leonard Cohen: Deaths and Entrances* (New York: Bloomsbury, 2021), 19.

4. Ira B. Nadel, *Leonard Cohen: A Life in Art* (Toronto: ECW Press, 1994), 91.

5. Simmons, *I'm Your Man,* 243.

6. In Paul Saltzman, "Famous Last Words from Leonard Cohen," *Maclean's*, June 1, 1972, archive.macleans.ca/article/1972/6/1/famous-last-words-from-leonard-cohen.

7. This film will be included in a five-disc retrospective box set of the 1972 tour, produced with Sony Music Entertainment and Sony Music Entertainment Canada Inc., due for release in 2023.

8. Harvey Kubernik and Justin Pierce, "Cohen's New Skin," *Melody Maker*, March 1, 1975.

9. Robert Enright, "Face Value: The Arts of Leonard Cohen, *Drawn to Words*" (Toronto: Drabinsky Gallery, 2007).

10. Ira Nadel, *Leonard Cohen,* 116.

11. Jason Ankeny, review of *I'm Your Man* by Leonard Cohen, *AllMusic,* allmusic.com/album/im-your-man-mw0000652083.

12. Jeff Burger, *Leonard Cohen on Leonard Cohen: Interviews and Encounters*, reprint edition (Chicago: Chicago Review Press, 2015), 215.

13. Simmons, *I'm Your Man*, 386–87.

14. Simmons, *I'm Your Man*, 425.

15. Anthony DeCurtis, "The Canadian Miserablist Returns with Rumbling Rumination on Sex and Love," *Blender*, web.archive.org/web/20040820035837/http://www.blender.com/reviews/review_911.html.

16. David Peloquin, "Leonard Cohen's Language of Symbolism," in Allan Showalter, "Leonard Cohen's Language of Symbolism: The Book of Mercy, Various Positions, and the Unified Heart," last modified May 5, 2020, allanshowalter.com/2020/05/05/leonard-cohens-language-of-symbolism-the-book-of-mercy-various-positions-and-the-unified-heart/.

## Land Acknowledgement

The Art Gallery of Ontario operates on land that is the territory of the
Anishinaabe (Mississauga) nation and is also the territory of the
Wendat and Haudenosaunee. The Dish with One Spoon Wampum Belt
Covenant is an agreement between the Haudenosaunee Confederacy
and the Anishinaabe Three Fires Confederacy to peaceably share and
care for the resources around the Great Lakes. Toronto is also governed
by a treaty between the federal government of Canada and the
Mississaugas of the New Credit (Anishinaabe nation). Toronto has
always been a trading centre for First Nations.

# Thank You

SIGNATURE PARTNER

GOVERNMENT PARTNER

SUPPORTING SPONSORS

The Art Gallery of Ontario is partially funded by the Ontario Ministry of Culture. Additional operating support is received from the City of Toronto, the Department of Canadian Heritage, and the Canada Council for the Arts.

Contemporary programming at the Art Gallery of Ontario is supported by

LEAD SUPPORT

The Dorothy Strelsin Foundation
Anonymous

GENEROUS SUPPORT

The Bloomberg and Sen families
Greg & Susan Guichon
Latner Family Foundation
Janice Lewis & Mitchell Cohen

ADDITIONAL SUPPORT

The Birks Family Foundation
The DH Gales Family Foundation

MEDIA PARTNER

Library and Archives Canada Cataloguing in Publication

Title: Leonard Cohen : everybody knows.
Other titles: Everybody knows
Names: Container of (work): Cohen, Leonard, 1934–2016. Works.
    Selections. | Art Gallery of Ontario, host institution, publisher.
Description: Contributors: Joan Angel, Laura Cameron, Julian Cox,
    Robert Kory, Alan Light, Michael Petit, Jim Shedden. |
    Catalogue of an exhibition held at the Art Gallery of Ontario
    beginning in December 2022.
Identifiers: Canadiana 20220429782 | ISBN 9781636810911
    (hardcover)
Subjects: LCSH: Cohen, Leonard, 1934–2016—Archives—
    Exhibitions. | LCGFT: Exhibition catalogs.
Classification: LCC ML410.C69 L46 2022 | DDC 782.42164092—
dc23

This book was published on the occasion of the exhibition
*Leonard Cohen: Everybody Knows*, organized by the Art Gallery of
Ontario from December 10, 2022, to April 10, 2023.

Published in 2022 by the Art Gallery of Ontario and DelMonico
Books • D.A.P.

Art Gallery of Ontario
317 Dundas Street West
Toronto, Ontario M5T 1G4
Canada
www.ago.ca

DelMonico Books
available through ARTBOOK |
D.A.P.
75 Broad Street, Suite 630
New York, NY 10004
artbook.com
delmonicobooks.com

Printed and bound in Belgium
ISBN: 978-1-63681-091-1

10 9 8 7 6 5 4 3 2 1

FRONT COVER:
Leonard Cohen
Self-Portrait II
1968
Instant print (Polaroid Type 20)
8.3 × 6.4 cm
Courtesy of the Leonard Cohen
Family Trust

BACK COVER:
Leonard Cohen
Self-Portrait *Photo Booth*
c. 1975
Gelatin silver print
20.5 × 5 cm
Courtesy of the Leonard Cohen
Family Trust

## Publication

EDITORS
Julian Cox and Jim Shedden

MANAGING EDITOR
Jim Shedden

PUBLISHING COORDINATORS
Robyn Lew
Kathryn Yuen

PRODUCTION AND
CONTENT EDITORS
Nives Hajdin
Kendra Ward

RESEARCHERS
Alex Arslanyan
Clint Enns

PROOFREADER
Judy Phillips

DESIGNERS
Gilbert Li, Alina Skyson,
and Sara Wong, from
The Office of Gilbert Li

PRE-PRESS
Paul Jerinkitsch

PRINTING
Type A Print Inc.

## Exhibition

CURATOR
Julian Cox

MANAGER OF
CURATORIAL AFFAIRS
Jill Offenbeck

PROJECT MANAGER
Melissa Ramage

INTERPRETIVE PLANNER
Gillian McIntyre

CURATORIAL RESEARCH
ASSISTANT
Alex Arslanyan

EDITOR
Nives Hajdin

EXHIBITION DESIGNER
Theodora Doulamis

GRAPHIC DESIGNER
Evelina Petrauskas

PRODUCTION
Malene Hjørngaard
Evelyn Quinn

## Exhibitions And Collections

CHIEF, EXHIBITIONS,
COLLECTIONS, & CONSERVATION
Jessica Bright

ASSOCIATE DIRECTOR,
EXHIBITIONS:
Laura Comerford

REGISTRATION
Alison Beckett, Cindy Brouse,
Jerry Drozdowsky,
Joel Herman, Dale Mahar,
Sabine Schaefer,
Curtis Strilchuk

COLLECTION INFORMATION
Alexandra Cousins,
Tracy Mallon-Jensen,
Liana Radvak,
Joe Venturella, Olga Zotova

CONSERVATION
Maureen Del Degan,
Christina McLean, Meaghan
Monaghan, Valerie Moscato,
Brent Roe, Rachel Stark,
Maria Sullivan, Tessa Thomas,
Joan Weir

LOGISTICS AND ART SERVICES
Gregory Baszun, Patric Colosimo,
Scott Cameron, Colin Campbell,
Brian Davis, Randal Fedje,
Tina Giovinazzo, Roland Hardy,
Iain Hoadley, Matthew Janisse,
Ruth Jones, David Kinsman,
Jason Laudadio, Alison Lindsay,
Paul Mathiesen, Angelo Pedari,
Craig Whiteside, Darin Yorston,
Tanya Zhilinsky

## Education & Programming

RICHARD & ELIZABETH CURRIE
CHIEF, EDUCATION &
PROGRAMMING
Audrey Hudson

DIRECTOR, ENGAGEMENT &
LEARNING
Paola Poletto

DIRECTOR, STRATEGIC
PROJECTS & OPERATIONS
Deborah Nolan

EDUCATION & PROGRAMMING
Danah Abusido, Madelyne
Beckles, Erica Chan, Maureen
DaSilva, Sarah Febbraro,
Nathan Huisman, Natalie Lam,
Idalette Martins, Kathleen
McLean, Zavette Quadros-
Evangelista, Annie Roper,
Melissa Smith

MEDIA PRODUCTION
Abbas Saifee, Matthew Scott,
Fraser Wrighte

—

## Development

CHIEF DEVELOPMENT OFFICER
Kate Halpenny

PHILANTHROPY
Rebecca Fera
Jane Hopgood

CORPORATE
Madeleine Dalkie

DONOR RELATIONS
Michelle Greenspoon
Matt Semansky

With a peacocks feather
I write this letter
It's like everything I do
Romantic and inept

This is A peacocks feather

Leonard Cohen, With a Peacock's Feather, date unknown

## Afterword: Leonard's Masterwork
Robert Kory

During the last decade of Leonard's life, I had the privilege and honour as his manager to assist him in realizing a final artistic dream. He had long been recognized as a poet, novelist, and songwriter of the first rank, but recognition as a performing artist had eluded him. That changed with his world tour of 2008 to 2013, which ranks as the most significant artist comeback of all time, and with his studio albums, *Old Ideas, Popular Problems,* and *You Want It Darker,* which all achieved number-one status in at least ten countries. No longer was Leonard a cult artist who filled small theatres; he became a worldwide icon who played in stadiums, with reviewer after reviewer nightly proclaiming their Leonard Cohen concert the best they had ever experienced.

When, in 2016, Leonard asked me to serve as the trustee of the Leonard Cohen Family Trust to manage his estate after he died, I accepted the role with little understanding of what lay ahead and with no expectation that Leonard would pass away later that year. In my role as manager while Leonard was alive, my focus was entirely on supporting his needs as a performing artist and in creating new work. That meant his focusing completely on the present and my assisting Leonard in avoiding entanglements of the past. He thrived creatively in a solitary environment, free from the obligations of friendship and custom, and fully present to a performing group that became a "musical family" with the mission of moving audiences every night as only Leonard knew he could. For me, the intense focus on his present performing and creative efforts came at the expense of gaining any understanding of Leonard's past. There was no time to talk about Leonard's then forty-year career, and he had no interest in it whatsoever.

How surprised I was, then, following Leonard's unexpected passing in November 2016, to learn during the first year of my trusteeship that all I had assisted him to achieve during my tenure as his manager paled in comparison to his completely unknown, true masterwork: his archive. In "Famous Blue Raincoat," Leonard implores his tormentor with the hope that "you're keeping some kind of record." That line, though largely unheralded, may be among Leonard's most important. He kept a record of his life as a multi-dimensional artist—poet, novelist, songwriter, visual artist, and performer—that ranks among the most complete of any modern artist. Only after his passing did I learn that Leonard had declared to his first biographer, Ira Nadel, that his archive was his real masterwork and that the published works were merely volcanic eruptions from the mountain, not the mountain itself.

So, my final duty to Leonard has been to organize an effort to digitize the entire archive—all 550 terabytes—with the intention that it may be made available for scholarship, exhibition, and preservation for future generations. The world of Leonard Cohen is far larger than we know, and I suspect it will take scholars decades to elucidate the brilliance of his unique work. Judy Collins, who first brought Leonard's songwriting to the public, has said his work reaches us in a place "so deep in our own spiritual development that we in turn benefit from his." There is no finer summary of why his work is worthy now and will be for generations to come. We have scratched the surface of his masterwork with this first exhibition at the AGO, intended to introduce his archive to Canada. If the recent past is prologue, then this initial inquiry into Leonard's archive will prove a first step in much more to come.

Leonard Cohen, *Self-Portrait with Mirrored Glasses*, 2009

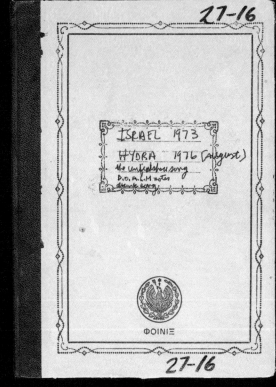
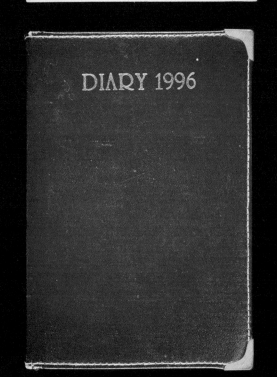
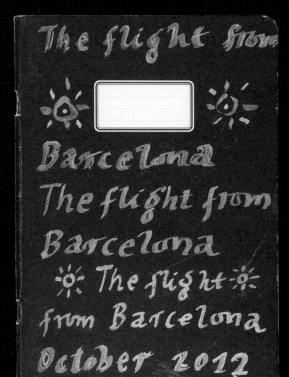